Country Music: New Poems

by

Dennis Cooley

(The Mackie Lecture and Reading Series, No. 2)

Cover design by Kalamalka Press.

Published in 2004 by
The Kalamalka Press
An imprint of the Kalamalka Institute for Working Writers
of Okanagan University College, 7000 College Way
Vernon, BC, V1B 2N5, Canada

National Library of Canada Cataloguing in Publication

Cooley, Dennis, 1944 –
***Country Music: New Poems* / Dennis Cooley.**
(The Mackie lecture and reading series ; 2)

ISBN 0-9693482-8-2

1. Prairie Provinces--Poetry. I. Title. II. Series: Mackie lecture and reading series ; no. 2.

PS8555.O575C68 2004 C811'.54 C2004-904815-5

Cover Illustration: Stone Wall, near Estevan, Saskatchewan, Fall 2002 by Dennis Cooley.
Author photograph: Dana Cooley.

Printed in Canada by Okanagan University College Print Services, Kelowna.

Dedicated to Diane
to the Mackie Gang-great hosts,
and to John Lent and Craig McLuckie-makers, friends.

Contents

Preface
Craig McLuckie
Chair, Kalamalka Institute for Working Writers

The Kalamalka Institute for Working Writers and The Mackie Lake House Foundation created the Mackie Lecture and Reading Series to fulfil part of the legacy of Mr. Patrick Mackie, a patron and practitioner of the Arts in this community. The Mackie Lake House is a component of the joint endeavour, where writers of all persuasions, unfettered by constraint, can bring a manuscript to completion while in residence.

The Kalamalka Press, noted for its past poetry competition, embarks on a new path: publication of this series of literary, cultural and creative writing, in any genre, by writers new and established, regional and international.

In addition to fulfilling part of Mr. Patrick Mackie's legacy, we intend to promote writing that considers the role of writing in contemporary society.

* * *

We are indebted to Professor Dennis Cooley and to our partners in this endeavour, the Mackie Lake House Foundation, especially to the energy and interest of Ms. Sharon Lawrence, Mr. Jamie Kidston and Ms. Tish Woodley.

Professor Dennis Cooley's contribution to this series was made possible by a SSHRC small universities grant, and the leadership provided by the OUC English Department's Chair, Dr. Kenneth Phillips.

Dennis Cooley's enthusiasm and deep love of literature is infectious, not least through his engaging performative readings: who else can read, dance a jig, and engage an audience on the subtelties of line breaks simultaneously! A Cooley *clamjamphry*[1] quickly emerged in the North Okanagan: John Lent and Jude Clarke, Craig McLuckie, Ross and Betty Jean Tyner, John and Shirley Murphy, Whitney and Pat Buggey, Sharon Lawrence, Alison Walker, Lexi Ratz, Annie Powter, and Kenneth and Suzanne Phillips among them. The *craïc* was great, *viz* Greg Simison's brilliant, self-deprecating performance of a nose tattooing. Diane Cooley is an exceptional person, a fine cook, and a considerate hostess; to her, our thanks.

Ms. Alexis Ratz, our very capable student intern at the KIWW, assisted with copy-editing and production. The SSHRC Small Universities Grant made Ms. Ratz' position possible. Ross Tyner, Craig McLuckie, John Lent and Alexis Ratz did multiple line copy-editing in our desire to ensure Cooley's intent:

> The poems are semantically dense, sinuous and irregular in lineation ... to allow room for eye and, room for the reader's psyche-to enter, engage, come up for breath, and re-enter them.

[1] Sometimes spelled *clamjamphrie*: a rowdy/unruly crowd.

> The space between pieces marks a rhythm of entrance and exit for the speakers too. The spaces between parts allow for readers to readjust as they move into new terrain, much of it unmarked in any easy or immediate way. It's crucial, I think, that there is room to step back, to wait, even to move elsewhere. The separations allow the parts to be marked as parts, as having some intactness of their own within the larger manuscript. As we move into different speakers, different voices, different domains, etc. the vertical holes more readily announce those shifts and invite readers to reset their time clocks. The gaps announce new hearings then, and allow for more varied expressive acts. This is especially true for the short, quiet pieces, which [are] set off with larger gaps leading into and out of them, but also with larger spaces within those pieces themselves.

Mr. Len Bidwell, Mr. Dan Sault and Mr. Christian Reiner, Okanagan University College Print Services, were and remain responsive printers and designers, whose work is of a high quality.

Now that this outlaw of Canadian poetry has completed *Country Music*, an homage to Estevan and Sinclair Ross's *As For Me and My House* (in part) in 131 sections, happy reading, resist "the marble orchard" and remember that *Mony wirds, muckle drouth*![2]

Cooley has, of course, ended with a promise—or a threat!:

      I've done my best
no no   there's no need for thanks

it is the least
      i could do
   it's not as if i thought
it was done
            or anything
    there there could be no more
not in the least

* * *

[2] Literally: many words make one thirsty.

Introduction to Dennis Cooley and *Country Music*
John Lent

> A poem tries to enact that wordless tumble and surge in its own medium—in line breaks and pauses, syntax and sound, the ripple and clarion strut of sense on the page. Through the nitty-gritty of craft, it tries to recreate the cadence of how things are...a poem thinks by the way it moves...there is a craft of scoring energy on the page.
> —Dennis Lee, "Body Music: Notes on Rhythm in Poetry"

> So the artist of abundancies [delights] in puns, interlocking and separating figures, plays of things missing or things appearing "out of order" that remind us that all orders have their justifications in an order of orders only our faith as we work addresses. Were all in harmony to our ears, we would dwell in the dreadful smugness in which our mere human rationality relegates what it cannot cope with to the 'irrational," as if the totality of creation were without ratios.
> —Robert Duncan, "Introduction," *Bending The Bow*

From the beginning of his prolific career as a poet in the mid-seventies, Dennis Cooley has engaged and extended the prosody/poetics of a strong vein of poets in this century that begins in these American voices—William Carlos Williams, Charles Olson, Robert Duncan and Robert Creeley—and extends through the influence of Robin Blazer and others into a strong Canadian tradition that includes, among others, George Bowering, bill bissett, Barry McKinnon, Fred Wah, Douglas Barbour, Ed Blodgett, Andy Suknaski, Robert Kroetsch, Daphne Marlatt, Dennis Lee, Anne Szumigalski and Cooley himself. This vein of prosody, beginning in the voices of Williams and Olson and Duncan, radically alters the notion of 'measure' in contemporary poetry, returning poetics to 'sound' as well as text, most specifically in the arduous notions of Williams' "natural phrase," Olson's "projective verse" and Duncan's "composition by field." These alterations in contemporary poetics—as dazzling, varied and contradictory as some of the results have been—have been resisted and under suspicion for almost one hundred years now. They represent a shift to the voices and rhythms of so-called ordinary people living their so-called ordinary lives, and that shift has been as political, as rich, and as complex as the shift from classical composition in music to the more open fields of notation developed by jazz musicians. The reader will experience one rich result of that shift in this volume of poetry and come to know it quickly, especially if the poems are read aloud. Dennis Cooley is one of our strongest composers from that point of view. He has worked at his craft with an almost urgent attention and hilarious sense of humour for over thirty years now, just like a seasoned old jazz pianist, refining his 'chops.' What most readers might *not* know as easily, however, is that Cooley has also been one of our most gifted articulators of this shift, and maybe, in at least one crucial way, through his carefully written essays on poetics, one of our most artful extenders of this shift into particularly new territory. In order to provide a solid context for reading these poems, I would like to make a few comments about his contribution from that point of view—Cooley as innovator.

Any reader of Cooley's poetry might greatly benefit from seeking out and reading the texts of two pivotal essays he has written on the formal aspects of the poetry he is advancing. The first of these essays is "Breaking and Entering (thoughts on line breaks)" and it opens up and explores the issue of abandoning formal poetic 'measure' and pursuing more unconventional, 'open' forms in poetry, especially in the writer's approach to line-by-line phrasing. In the end, Cooley places the move towards 'composition by field,'—the loose, improvised, jazz-like play between text and space, sound and silence, logic and whimsy—in the context of postmodern thinking about art. By allowing the poetic text to assume a spatial rather than temporal logic and measure, the poem not only returns poetry to the 'singing' that it began in centuries ago, but it also operates politically in the sense that it both de-centers received order and logic and demands the reader's participation. This essay explains why a poet might take the approach Cooley has taken in *Country Music* to the important relationship between word and graphic space, that constant, joyous exploration of the 'measure' of the mind and body being alive, or, as Lee says, 'the craft of scoring energy on the page.'

The second essay readers might consult is "The Vernacular Muse in Prairie Poetry," an essay that indicates, in its politics and its vision, the extent to which Cooley is an innovator as well as a practitioner of a new kind of prosody. The essay begins by allowing all of the critical voices that have dismissed this kind of poetry, and in particular, the 'flat' voices of its prairie practitioners, to have their say. Cooley quotes extensively from outrageously dismissive reviews of his own poetry in order to show just how misunderstood this kind of poetry *is*, especially by those critics and other poets who have clung to a kind of high-modern formalism. Then, in an incredible feat of unrelenting momentum, he proceeds to demonstrate how important the 'vernacular' voice actually *is* in our lives, how important it is to use it, celebrate it, let it loose among its equally 'vernacular' things like cars and horses and towns nine miles apart and nuisance grounds and drive-ins...the endless density of the lives we actually *lead* as opposed to the sanitized versions of those lives so often represented in other kinds of modern and postmodern poetry. From Bakhtin to Derrida to Genette to Jakobson to Eagleton to Foucault, Cooley proceeds to hammer home what an incredibly political *entity* the vernacular voice in art actually *is*. He is as eloquent, as complex and as passionate about this issue as Wayman is about the importance of hearing people's *real* voices, especially people at work. And it is here, in his celebration of the vernacular voice, in his insistence upon it, that Cooley extends his own lineage from the point of view of Williams, Olson and Duncan. In their wake, Cooley has become the wiley postmodernist, post-colonialist, post-structuralist, abandoning the grand narratives and obsessions with mythology that mark some of Olson and Duncan's poetry, and has moved toward the crazy, layered, spatial epics of the here and now, *this* place, *this* now, in all its polyhrythmic, polyphonic and polyglossic texture.

It seems strange in some ways to have to introduce the poetry of *Country Music* in this way, but, as I mentioned earlier, Cooley is inviting the reader to listen to a different kind of music, surrender to the rhythms and complexities of jazz, say, after only being exposed to the more formal rhythms and complexities of classical music. And with the delightful result, possibly, of discovering that this new music is, both ironically *and* deliberately, closer to the physical and psychological rhythms of our day to day lives and thoughts, or, as Lee says, the 'cadence of how things are.'

In the poetry of *Country Music* the reader will find a vintage combination of what I've mentioned above: open, loose, improvised forms delivered in a vernacular voice that insists the reader roll up his or her shirtsleeves and join in. There'll be no sitting in a chair at *this* dance, passively watching the rest of the community gliding around the hall to "Goodnight Irene" or any other of these reels and breakdowns.

&

the world rolled by
like a playbill
in dogwood speed
when the bunch of them
philip phyllis steve paul jude
jumped onto the paper as it wound by
wondered about trips to another land
hoped in the ravines of their lives
to be transported
taken by surprise

&

think of you there echoes
/theatre of their emptiness

slats i sit inside
alone among the flats
afraid to stand up
knowing when i do

the seat will make
a terrible racket

there ill be there
youll be
shuffle-footed under a red-faced moon
where it has clambered to the top
and now it's stuck
it can't get off
the posters they have pasted on every corner
talk about glamour

wonder if you will find me
on deck silting the sea with darkness
fitting for the role if you will
give me half
a chance if i can
win the part i most want
when you say my god you are
one good looker and i say
well that's what you do
isn't it you poets you are always
into everyone's pockets & you say
as a matter of fact no you say

every night the stars switch on
& there is a loud clamour
that's when the moon goes
ballistic i mean let's get real
is tick all that's left when
the show hits the road
that's when things start
to happen that's when
the fun begins

hours you say shall be
a night in shining amour

well you say
do you want it
or not

&

town torn in half
a theatre ticket ript
before it starts before you know
the parts a long tear
where the CPR stretches
its broad stitches down the middle

the train rips through
every monday every tuesday every
wednesday thursday friday they all
are through days every single saturday
sunday afternoon the way out a wound that closes
a zipper the train pulls shut behind

pool elevator a heart lying there
in the night that is its own dark blood

&

now you have
gone I step
into darkness
the yard holds heavy as water
yawns & swallows

blind
where i look back   the house
its tank full of light
the yard waits, all ocean & night
a slow swish swish *wish wish*

teeter there
the gate on the house
light pulls in yellow yarn
light weeps a valve my heart keeps
blood going past
a canal that never fills
fills so full it runs over
a cranial nerve/ pulled
could be a wound and there is no salve

`you somewhere      out there`
`lone as a cow   a stone   a crow`
`the pasture filling   with moonlight`

&

blur on the horizon
you lean in blue
-gray but do not advance
in the cornsyrup air you cannot pass
lines from sun
snag & stick you are
suspended
on the rim of the world
its red clay
about to cave in
at your feet what looks like
a slough of water

you slouch inside the heat
your approach a delay
reproach to the ending
i am waiting for

you are stuck in a trough of light
a fly dragging through butter
day a torn blotter
threatens to disintegrate

you walk as though drugged
your words wading through
begin to slur

sway in slow
motion I do not know
when or if
over the hot slate of sky
you dare not touch
if ever you will arrive

inside the prairie at 100^0
bugs drowning
we wait in pockets of heat

&

Paul could & he did
up & unzip
his dreams boy oh boy could he ever
snip snip & zap his fantasies fall open
quick as a blizzard from alberta
come rain or shine he is bound & determined

Paul tugs `Saturday Night`
through his shaving
kit takes pain to pull
soap cream razor
lotion romance the whole kit & kaboodle
all he's ever wanted every wish turned

inside out   a sock at night
the brush in his hand blooms
beautiful as russian thistle

PAUL KIRBY
MAN ABOUT 5 ft 4

the letters say in embossed enthusiasm
& he is mad about
now he's washed up
he is about
to kick up his heels
shoot he's about
the best damn thing to hit town
since '22 when the chinook blew in
for a whiskey

Canuck Kirby hauls his outfit out of the place
the palaces in his mind where cowboys are cowboys
riding through sage and sunburn past porches and barns
riding through verandahs parlours and pianos
that play at rescue
Paul Kirby admires himself lean as dogs leg in the previews
up mesas down canyons pinafores mountains
that look as though they were added in purple crayon
patches of fescue phyllis finds, pointing
hay where'd those things come from /buzzards

p. yawning in the credits where light is coming up
riding the ravine his pinto through dust & smoke
where ladies lead wild rose or prim rose
lives ox-eye daisies & wild camomile
in white sleeves & camisoles sigh
the days' ease at either end

Paul opens the novel where he has kept the cowboys
grins the heroes shrugs & slouches are folded
          / / bookmarks in the story
Paul has kept them reliable & dogeared as promises
     neater than the violets Phyllis has
thought of filling her copy of Swineburne with
Paul reaches in like Mandrake shakes out the red
bandanna rehearses the lines smooths
them with his hands he's hung on
a peg in the story he's carefully
     sawn & nailed together

jimminy creepers Paul thinks
as he heads to town   to town heads he
hell-bent for chiasmus up one chasm
down another crevasse
drawn to deep cracks in the surface
brownness rich & loud in him
tan browner than nicotine
his horse moving firm & confident
stoically through the open
snow in a silent film
he leads with his chin

&

My Dearest Philip,   my dearest

something in me Philip
I am sorry to have to something growing like a tumour only
bother you like this, I its not a frog a lizard
hope it's ok, but there might be a bird even I dont know
is something I have to the way theres a flutter I am sick
tell you, Philip, and it is Mr. _________s eye it is
there's no one else I you Philip you have entered me
can go to. Please meet & now I can't shake you though what
me at the trestle at 8, ever you I do you float off like the
I know Phyllis will be moon as cold & white whatever I say

out. Please come I want you clench in my flesh
like a worm I need to talk with you see you bad

My Love,   my love,
Jude.   Jude.

&

meeting you
like this
: the air between
steps between wanting
possibly waiting who can tell
so steep i lose my footing
carry my wanting
in my left hand it bounces
a small hurricane
let loose in weather

lantern in wind *hurryhurry*
hurt that will never go out
no matter what or where
i go out to meet you
clasp burning my throat

so tenacious
it cries in its box
& night grips
could be the nail that holds
you at the lectern

and why not why not
when i think of you
thick with body
i wish we could

carry ourselves off
i could be you
a travelling shoe
salesman or chat
auqua singer
one who loves
to travel
be carried away
when life is an acquifier

the cool & shining
we pass through
we acquire

&

Steve his nose
running wipes the back
with his mitten skids
when he hangs
onto the sleigh
his hands must be frozen

jing jing jing jing jing

rides the tracks and then
swoops
out wide
when the horses turn
Mr. Marklinger not looking doing it for him

the cold jingling
their breath in little jets
backs steaming where they quicken reluctantly
in small sizzles snow sprays and
I love the feel
my cheeks cold and I expect
red from watching

Steve out at the end

hey looket mom looket

trying not to be flung
hoping he will
his voice clear in the air
where it is losing light

so dazzling this afternoon
when we lift across the whiffs of snow
and the doughnut glaze the thin crust
where it's melted we had to
close our eyes
against the light

Steve streams into a softening blue
his cap the muffs proudly up
mittens that will be crusted
with frozen breath and snot
swirls under a moon that watches
pale as a polished bone
the stars about to reassemble
from sky to sky
their hard cold light

&

you and your secret
life is
a box of peaches
eyes pry open
all the way from the okanagan

your squeaks of resistance
hopes for romance beyond all reaching
speak of consistence
surprise when it happens
shock that it happens
at all

&

July was for
ever was full
was wind & sky &
forever & forever a fever
in me, us
days & days to get there
& never arrive

the sparrows
sorrow long as bows as spare
for all their quickness
saying *fever fever*
quirky little things

the five trees on fire
the small elms seething
take in the summer

chlorophyll drips
in little gusts

green air we gather
under & drink ,huge
quart sealers
so cold they fog up
grateful for green for cool
for trees that burn into eternity

July a windy fever in us

&

please Mr. Fuller
Brush man make me
fast as you can make me
fuller & fuller
full as you can
brush all the lint off & out
& no fooling

do not
give me
the brush off

you can give me the once   *couldn't fail*
over the touch up the rush   *to feel her*
till I am rushed   *nerves speed*
off my slippered feet   *runs like a well*
warm with dare   *oiled sewing machine*
slippery with desire

the way i imagine you
lean over you have
learnt this somewhere & you
& i put   how this fuels her
out feelers dreams small enough but
feel dreams against   they have seen such failures
warm like the teapot
my thoughts   that they could fool me

imagine
me loud as an old clock
newly cleaned newly oiled
oil & lint built up in its belly
button button who's got the button
I say
you hit the button
you do it's
there right be
tween your hands
all the brands you hand me

& just when you think
well you got things
sewn up pretty much
if i were to bite
sticks sometimes   the thread off
when it gets too thick   I would drop (love)
into your lap

& you like me
sent spinning
might lose
your footing
for good
or bad

&

o westryn wynde

rain when it comes :
when wilt thou blow

if it were to
arrive i imagine would be

some ocean blue in places
and fish as if kids have
finger-painted them and they
wedge into night onto ledges
pose as parrots turn yellow
and orange as carrots and
they rub against white and
it would be so green it
would shine like a basin
like soda straight from the
bottle the sky radiant with
pomade & oysters in the
shell

and when it does
rain that is
the small rain down doth rain
it will be cold
needles of a sewing
machine and it will raise
braille on the fields

remove the stem to our brains
the soft beating of 8 billion legs
grasshoppers drowning in deluge

just now this doesn't
happen this is not
going to happen
christ if my love were in my arms
when i look into the sky at night
all the bits of light enamelled there
hard shiny insects
strewn in periods & commas
dull clinks when they pop against the sky

i can see the whole creation
know that all day sky will get skinny & warp the sun
squirt oil into our eyes
that always it will knock out our sight
wrap us in a plastic that is close and sticky

the days sting us to a brown forgetting

and i in my bed again

&

not much I know but the Wheelers
burnt out fourth year running
they take the brunt of this, the farmers

in the meantime we've got to make the best
of it and so I think a horse why a horse
Paul why not a camel say

we could highstep the sand in camel bells and caravans
sounds of lambs in our ears and goats, the bells
sharp smell of goats, sweeter than iambs even
their cheese we're not ill fated man snap out of it
do I have to draw a picture don't you know
the way we could sidestep the Mucklers step
out as if we were born to it, the alacrity of wrens
hands full of caramel sunlight the sweet electricity

there would be
the yellow slant of September fragrance of camomile
wed be wed wed be Anthony & Cleopatra
all over again
we could you know, practically
horny as thorns that brush against nights somewhere
it would be a night in shining
amour we'd be
in clover all over again you know we would
everything sleek as silk comely as camisole stockings

think of it there you'd be the sheik of estevan
a bedouin even & me id say
whose bed you in huh you could be
this handsome and chique stranger
young girls would shriek and giggle
you could be a gigolo but I wouldn't
let you I wouldn't let you
out of my sight, ever
id go for shacking up
no slacking whatever gig
you played

just think, no more thin things
it would be dates & figs nothing but
figs & dates forever everything

coming up the rest of our lives
up one sand dune and down the other

saying one good sand dune deserves another
kiss what have we done to deserve this
forget the faces full of vinegar we can have a little fun

&

when he sees my startled face
look p. says look
stoops to the rail
what am i on trial or what
this is on the trestle
the train has just clanked past
has wrestled something out of the ground
or to you can't be sure
what/
is he a dwarf and i snow white

trust me he says

we can still
feel
the trembling
& he kneels

at first i think
it's the sound
he wants me
to hear where it's climbed over the steel
ear he lays on the shining
line he is listening for ponies
peonies blooming in his ear
man at the fair the pennies between
his fingers blossom
open & shut

or the long long sound of its going
sounds of cities it has cried
when it passed over head
& it sets off tuning forks
other places in you forever

but this time
he reaches
& reaches to me

here he says,
faces drifting off their edges
& when he sees
I hesitate
says ,for your thoughts
go ahead, it's yours

there in my palm
shiny & warm
the king's face squashed & drifting
the man in the moon
lifting a weather balloon
into the early evening

&

every morning my heart in hiding
a wet red thing huge with grief
warty with waiting

in my mind all night long this stranger
comes riding riding riding
straight out of my heart
right out of the frame
each morning rises near as flame
right out of the blue there he is
famous as jesus
himself in his jeans

a broken finger, wagon,
what can I say, I don't know
low and rheumatic in love
pneumatic in bliss in breathing
i am concerned believe me
through & through

though i have always fancied myself
an equestrian me
who should have
squandered everything   thoroughly
sequestered myself west of home   or east
fear now I will ride gravely a final carriage
the last cartilage torn loose

HOWDY he says he has come to meet me
in the mirror in the naughty mirror he grins
HOWDY his vest says and cool
as an unspent cartridge he steps
out of the glass
edges the blue won't hold

the bevelled room
all the stars you are holding
are breaking   out in your skin
you a high
way man you hand
some devil you ride
your way up the gravel
up to the old in door

&
hadda i hear now five now five
now fi hear fi who make it fi'ty
fitly we wait on shore & some wade out

shrill seagulls feeding &
grasshoppers move in like minnows

fi' fifty fi' fifty now d'ahve five fifty
Colin Zimmerman calls down the end of time
& we stand by   press on
fearing the world will go
down in fire or up
in dust it must be
presbyterian

the lord sure as hell's been practising the old bugger
dust to dust from here to eternity & back
nothing but eternity here to the correction line
more like it & we are in
deep up to here is what

rust to rust too though how on earth harrows
could rust in the middle of a desert is beyond me
harrows or any other damn thing
only thing we lack is
scorpions & adders
though the banks seem full of them

this here next lot ladies & gentlemen
real fine lot hold 'er up there Gabe
so's people can get a look linens sheets
pillow cases real fine table cloth
all the way from Ontario in the family for years
hand-stichin' take a looket this lovely coat
Mrs. Joseph she done 'er herself

it is only year after year blows washes away
time irons lines into the linen and into
all the faces that once did lie on it

ok now who'll gimme four gimme four askin' four

Evie Josephs stands there so forlorn
the kids beside her thin & jumpy as grasshoppers
watch with those eyes from which everything's thrown
overboard into the wake we commemorate
the flotsam and jetsam of their passing

trunks with dents & missing handles letters from down east asking about
kids and crops dinner plates with blue flowers and chips ploughs that lean
forlornly in wind hoes seed grain side tables harness that's worn nearly
through cream separators with red handles and big bowls kerosene lamps
crocheted table cloths moths have gotten to meat grinders all thrown
overboard beds that sag chests of drawers that say they are gone hay
hooks christmas cards with snowmen and sleighs that horses pull tinkling
up lanes lined with elms and say may the joy of the season brighten your
home wooden churns tangled twine chains pitchforks with rough handles
sewing baskets swathers a keg of nails half empty horse shoes curry
combs with horse hair in them cream cans a picture of a dutch windmill
the oak table they brought all the way from ontario first married all tossed
to the winds such a terrible feeling the tides taking them the wind
whapping our faces

lean like lost mariners into wind
the house gray for years now beached
everything bleached whatever
bends away from wind and spume
blown into faces gritty with dirt
we can hear the strain in the rigging
think of nails when they're pulled

we're all blown up on a sandbar & the water's dropping
the barn where it's cut adrift comes undone in storm
already filling up with emptiness where creatures stand
in puzzled & terrified eyes
all that can be remembered barnacled below the surface
barn floats off with the terrible screams
horses & pigs & cows
bellowing somewhere beneath eternity

It will surely hold in the straits of fear
When the breakers tell that the reef is near;

Though the tempest rave and the wild winds blow,
Not an angry wave shall our bark o'erflow.

the seas open and
they drown
not a boat in sight

dog by the door knows she is already alone
sees behind her abandonment
the kids & kettles cling
like insects on the bennett buggy
the family sets sails very
slowly disappears
in a clunk of pots and pans
behind two ribbed & bitten horses
in the sand leave two
long tracks of an enormous creature
that takes them over the horizon to somewhere
near extinction

&

hold up your face a storm
lantern you search
the dark for dark
faces lost in the room
at the table you want
to fall upon
& illumine

you will rub sadness off
so they will shine back

they orbit you, faces
drift in your direction
dazzled, dazed

feel of sitting behind
the moon the dark side

now you are
not here where you are
dark wind of emotion

shone in it myself once
even when you were not by

only now your face wobbles
toward other planets
ether of their movement

at the end of your arm
your face
fills all the corners
more lively than lightning
lovely with the bright face you turn now
always away

&

it was a hot day hot and dusty
fenders so hot you could barely
trace your name the day
they nailed Jesus nailed him to a letter
it was you might say a red letter day
bang bang they said take that
they said they got him to a T
& we in turn wept in our model lives
our model-T hands modestly clenched
drove all our suspicions home, envy too
backfired with every teapot word
pop pop you're dead & swept eyes
over the faces of the dead
land detected sin there still
knew when the thing moved
our hands telling we had found it
hounds under the step lank & panting
sun a burning lemon

our hair is grieving our bones
remember all we didn't do
restless with regret with grass
hoppers that leap from their folding
chairs hope to clear the promenade

phosphorous more & more on our breath
we dream of his gentle rough hands
carpenters hands
so soft they could soothe another
year or quicken to joy
where night & day join, aching

this man we follow to the elbow
observe everything to the letter
we're dressed to the nines &
we nail him with our anger
split him like a T-bone
spittle coming from the mouth
that's the spirit we tell
each other our spite
hard as railway spikes

invite him to a tea come in we say
to a hole days drain into
takes us with it

take that we say & we hammer
home the point take another sip
of tea under the parasol swirl
& gulp the lemonade smile
through our long & yellow teeth
take that we say
we got you where we want you
you son of a bitch
we have a stake in this too you know
all of us into total abstinence
teetotalers to the end

the faint sucking noise
when we gnaw on his bone

had him where we wanted
jesus did we ever

&

know what it is
to be a sewing
machine its little runs
& slows
runs & slows
so easy

Singer 338 Complete Service

√ **clean & oil**
√ balance tension
√ check timing
√ set zero clearance
√ adjust needle bar height
√ set winder clutch washer
√ correct foot control

Thank You

Hank Singer

thankyewthanthankyewthankyewthankyewthankyewha
nkyew

&

me ms. bentley a bent rib
he plays his music on
morning noon & night
a wet ache
between his calls
too real when i feel
what my heart can't conceal
I like to play with the horn
I took from him
all the hurt & lost amity
lost love & loneliness
sea of heartbreak I'd sing like crazy

it's a heartache nothin but
a heartache when the moon
hits your eye like a big pizza pie
your cheatin' heart he said
will tell on you you don't
know what it's like
don't let the stars
get in your eyes
if I ain't got you babe
it's only a paper moon

Listen Mr. Adam I would say
I would have to
give the devil his dew
it isn't my fault you were so hasty
so you don' need tuh get nasty
I got a bone to pick with you too you know

don't you know anything
is what I would say
Where's the garden yuh bin
promisin', huh? ain't that
a shame yr the one to blame

and then id say

you made me cry when you said good bye
hey that's no way to say goodbye
all those catchy words
they're the ones id speak

there id be

standin in the pourin' rain
ribbon of darkness over me
I'd sing my face off I'd sing
like there was no tomorrow
pretending that you're still around

and one other thing

: will you still love me tomorrow?

&

winter
& the sky
so huge so creaky
sun & snow
bright where you walk
coyotes talk to themselves
close their eyes against the light

Christmas morning
you are coming to dinner
the smell of turkey roasting
the sharp tang of mandarin

& nuts when you crack
you pull out their small brown brains
& you say phyllis
would you like one
the knubby feel in your hand

you are coming
where this morning the smell of coffee
hits like a blessing
the way when philip says
may the love of jesus christ
& the peace that passeth understanding
be with you now
& ever more
& then we sing prolonging the moment
aaaa men
aa aa men aaa aa aaa aa men

though I do not believe
& I do not think Philip believes
it quickens me always to tears

this morning
on the window the frost
grows a white forest
blazing with sun
& I know I will see you

lo, he says, I will be
with you
alway

&

no one knows why but everyone knows
one day when the sky is
shoved to one side
the cartilage will pop &

the sun will fall
it will tumble out of a chamber in the sky
turn white & explode

some day it will stop
stars that have stopt

shining in all these countries all these
centuries in our hands &
for all their slippage constant

one day someone will turn
a knob on the cupboard

we have kept the oil & vinegar in
one day these things will happen

everything at the edges glowing
one day a hand

will open the door
and the shelves will take a deep breath

will feel a moment cooler
not know what, quite

one day it will

one day i will
take down the stars you have
hidden under the stairs like cartridges
put at the back of the cupboard pull
open the door behind
see where the sun shines quietly
among the pickles & butter

i will if you let me
open your hands
rub them with oil
small jar i have kept

next to the sky just before
it starts to end

&

going
the other way
sssshh^ee wwwww they'd say
szze^eww
& they'd be
long gone
/likethat
like dogs on speed
like giant mosquitoes
but there was only the one
and it would flash
everything else pulled to the side
pullets waiting in dust
& the air bullied past

before you knew it it would be gone
and i would cluck & wonder
what were they doing
where were they going
was it somewhere

there is water and lights on water

and then i would feel
as if i reached
failed to catch
my balance &

hit my head on ice
there would be a long thunnnkk
when it passes
the wire that
kept the cows out or in

though not the crows
the crows knew and they would step through or around
the trick of electricity &
they would listen   at the door
is that so   don't say   is that so
tip their heads to the thick wet heads

&

it's the square dance birdie
fly out & crow fly in & you
dance in giddy as a bride a bear
in saskatoons we are
dancing you & I & all
over june it's crazy & then

we are waltzing just us
as if we had always
we are waltzing the turns
we surrender ourselves to
come completely unbridled
touching each other & yes
the sweet turns it takes

blue were the skies and blue were her eyes
and blue were the blue skirts she wore

all this: the oak floor, our faces, shining
benches chairs eyes doors

me holding you holding me
& we dance, dance through corners

you & I you & I
move with what is in us
till you would think we careen
boats on the water bumping
soft hair on your neck
faces so close we lose focus

varnished faces, vanish as if
we sanded them away
bumps in the floor

& always the heat of your body
under my hand, changing,
your face is your face is & we are

we are dancing always
always we are dancing
we are always

dancing,
my darling, we are
dancing
& the floor the floor is

moving
under

&

No way I was makin' an early exit to the marble orchard, drought or no drought. No blinkin' way I'm gonna kiss 'er goodbye, if it was the last thing I did.

Other people goin' under easy as potatoes, people droppin' like spiders through the cracks and bugger all anybody's doin' about it, know what I mean? If it happened once it happened a thousand times.

Ever tell you bout the time I go on welfare? Walk around the town hall 6, 7 times, the whole block this is, wear a path deep as buffalo on their way to oblivion. 'M tryin' to do it, go in & do it. Finally make 'er in & to make a long story short here's this old school chum of mine, he's got this job with a yellow pencil. Goddamn wonder how he knows which end to hold.

"Listen, McLuckie, I gotta tell yuh somethin'" Yellow Pencil says. There he sits, under the face of the goddamn King Hisself, and tells me without a word of a lie. "Don't let them catch you in the beer parlour is all." Beer parlour? What is this—beer parlour? I mean you know me, whenever do I go near the goddamn place? "Well, all right, but some bastard spotted Alan Avery way over in Shaunavon and that was it. One word and they're off welfare, wife and three kids, little one still in diapers. Justlikethat. No if's, but's, or maybe's, that's it, they've had it. Just thought you should know, that's all." Yellow Pencil taps, tap tap tap, edge of the table. Not his fault, only tryna help. I don' let out a peep, he can tell I'm peeved. "Just watch it eh, that's all I'm saying Craig." He slams the register shut like a strongbox.

"By the sweet Jesus you can't mean it," I say. "Surely to Christ they wouldn't do a thing like that."

Just looks at me. "It's a bugger, McLuckie," he says.

Well that floored me, put near. Musta noticed coz he sez "Oh yeah, another thing."

Another thing?

"Yeah. Yr liquor permit."

"Permit?"

"Uhhuh. Fraid I gotta take yr liquor permit off of you. Sorry, Craig, beats me why but they're real tough-nosed bout that." And me I'm standin' there like a kid kept in after school. Forty-two-year-old man on welfare, what choice he's got? Hell, what choice 's anybody got? And you just stand there and you don't know what the hells happened, what's happening to you.

Well no worsern anybody else I guess when you think of it. Head off to her place soon's I can get outa there, bin a while since I bin there, so dang hot it'll burn holes clean though the boots you don't watch it, and I pop around the side, out of the wind sorta. And be damned there isn't this sudden patch of brightness, middle of weeds yea high, talk about bright, this is bright with a capital B, these flowers will hurt your eyes you ain't careful.

And there she is, Phyllis & her tin water & all them flowers gulping all she can pour down their gullets.

This in the middle of the bald-headed prairie, so help me god, sun so nasty you gotta watch it don't tear the soles off of yr boots. You know what I'm talkin', dust so bad you can't see the front door, grasshoppers, they've ate up the Eaton's catalogue in the outhouse, every last page, even the glue, no shit. And winds. Where they come from, and why, who knows, but they just keep rubbin' rubbin' rubbin', these dry strong winds, day after day, heat, all night long so you can't think, you flap like a tent and as dry. Holy Moses she's one big woodstove, the prairies.

I'd shove the wind around if I could but not Phyllis, here she is, stringy as a range-fed hen, she's pouring her heart out and there it is, big bright splashes at her feet, flowers all over hell's half acre, and she has names for all of them you can't imagine.

What's really funny is she's wrapped like a Bedouin & this here is her garden. Her garden smack in the desert. Dark dark eyes look out, woman could pop the eyes out of a statue, know what I mean? "Oh, hello Mr. McLuckie," she says. More relief in that little garden than the whole kit and kaboodle they trot out at the town office & call it relief let me tell you.

&

rrrrrrrr-rrrrrrrr-rrrrrrrr-rrr

someone cranking
voices inside the phone
kerosene lamp its gentle talk
a yellow shore i sit

knit knit knit

pull the yarn into small bridges
someone giving up on grief

hello i say *hello*
hello you say ***hello***

i say *is it you*
3 long, 1 short
are you there

something acid on the air
acrid in my ear
katie angus listens in anger
hopes for a pool of scandal
her eyes grow bright
wanting to wring gossip out of the phone
watches the receiver as if it were a sun
dial to heaven
small joys trickling out of the oak into her ear

one day we can only hope in the sweet by and by
she will pass out from too much rumour

&

all night long the ragweed is shrinking
flowers closing their throats
thirsty for morning its yellow oil
weeping into the yard the goose tapping
her loneliness at the pane

imagine you out there
the long windy night
the long purple nerves
wiring us together

&

this is what they say the men
whose lives choke them
throats in collars

religion a harness on these honest folk
what they say a mustard plaster on their breathing
men so burnt they have turned to charcoal
have turned blunt as an anvil angels beat on
frogs flattened on the road
if you can find any
frogs that is

say we got what we deserved this is what we get
for sin will go on & on & on upon the face of the earth
there's no stopping sin once she gets a head up
cold hail heat wind lightning grasshoppers
it's all too good for us they say
—and that's not counting husbands

say we wait for a garden one that is
wet with noses lit with lilies
so lush we will walk naked again
(only they do not say this
I have read this in philip's book
and there were pictures)

fair enough heavens I can hardly
wait let's get on with it why don't we
I could go for the lilies and roses
I could go for that part
they say it is the Dirty Thirties
what about ours, I could try that, I'm thirty-some,
enough of the thrifty enough of the collar
let's snap to it let's find a horse of a different colour
how about sucking on something sweeter, huh
how about it huh aincha interested
playing dirty i mean
aawww c'mon
/jist a little bit
thirty or no thirty I'm terribly thirsty
could use a snort

just wait'll the ladies get wind of this
why not thistles

is all we have to clutch
P's epistles to the heat
all the hearts infested with prickles
preserved like pickles in brine

&

that man from Beechy
so help me god
that's right

that is the place
only from such a name
could we hope
anything could
happen

it all fell out

his cool cool eyes

must have known the secrets of fish
the way they go, gloves full of water
holding themselves, cold on the grand banks
so thick sailors once said you could walk on them
they said he could see things seethings sea things
seeping from the arctic a kind of solicitude they thought
he was past all soothing Sukanen they said his name was
Finnish and that too seems right a Finn with fish
on the brain holding himself
against or within
solitude so things could be

to go and do a thing like that
they say he banged together an ark
dreamt he would drag his dreams
across an alien desert
1,027 miles one bay one ocean
make his way home in a bandage
: huge bug on water

till the small moisture in him hurtled
his mind disappeared beneath the keel
deep inside leather under wood underneath
the thirst the prairie yanked out in handfuls

and he dug in
the earth became

a telescope he peered through
became a badger only bigger
watched our dry hopes surf past
year after year billowed around him

Philip said he walked a thousand miles
it must have been like walking on water
& it was, surely, the way he looked
curing in the pickled light

curious how that man had home in his head
held it under bone struts
unletting as a pit bull

think of it the water must have been
hammered blue as the seas in his eyes
a red & brown sky they say
so blond he could be the land itself
grown blind under ground
when at last he emerged
there was urgence in his days

&

she is

he knows

a place

he comes to

a smoothness of dates a sin
            fullness that is pears & nut
meg moons roll woodenly overhead

by day alkali flakes off the sun
dissolves fizzing in water they drink

& then the sweet water he stumbles upon
when he rattles through stubble
                  & there she is   /still
   as an egret

            half-blind from
    heat & drifting
ruined from regret
            where rain falls
forms cataracts of darkness
   some kind of
      loneliness

&

he says & the rest of us
lean closer into the radio
shelter in the sounds
coming out its windows

a genuine 1932 GE cathedral radio
wish we could step inside
its cool corridors its dusky musings
want the simple reassurances

knock
            knock **knock**

it says who's there & then
                  it says

we-eLL co-ommmm
IN!

keep happy with the happy gang
because when you're happy
& you're healthy
to heck with being wealthy

he says & we lean
further in

&

every spring & every fall
birds flow down
the sky, vast & vascular
an open thorax
the whole world bleeding

& all the time in dry grass a ticking
time makes fire as it lies there or rises

they dig holes bore hollows
down into the light & through it

there in the sandy soil
a small hill seeded with stones
talk rises from alyssum sweet
mustard plastered on day

till they fill up with darkness
till there are wells & there
is loneliness splashing
we lie in till we drown
eyes rinsed clean as bone

flown out to the dark before the dark
& we cross the darkness like water

are touched by god see things
graveyards at night a lithium moon
cool as asylum clear as the angel
who for ten thousand thousand years
stands there on knees & bright toes, staring

&

touch me touch
oh me yes oh

sweet jesus
touch me

&

asses to asses
lust to lust

hard to assess hard to access
paul says when philip says you have to
wonder it makes you wonder
word without end
heaven to goodness yes
he has something

to say lay
Ds and gentle
men the world will end
at exactly 12 midnight
12:30 in newfoundland

says it's true it will there must be
a lot of holiness then
the whole place 's become a sandbox
we're digging holes and falling in
look at the goldurn fields
they're seeded with souls
far as he could see
sifting in under the door
round the windows till all the sills are coated
glory be to hello lou yeah
though they seemed to have lost
a bit of their lustre and now they've
drifted up to the tops of fenceposts
crow says hey aint that heaven blowin' by now
: clouds of dust clouds of glory
crow loving tropes
wearing toupees she calls nests

yippee yi yo yippee yi yey

the cowboys call the one
last round-up

the prairie a big red
church everywhere a coming & going
the face of the earth
our faces too
face it this is true
grit we being quiet
with watching
glowing with dust
we learn to armwrestle the wind
crouch under the trestle when it shakes
jake on his rusted machinery
insists is a host of angels
los angelos hadn't we heard
haven't we heard don't we know
/anything

for pete's sake
there can be no amnesty
not when they are ringing in the end of time

)you cannot be saved
by the bell not when god is
bringing in his herds

below all reckoning 200 steers
their dust and bellowings
shitting themselves with fear

&

want to know how I feel
how wobbly with want I can get

one of those turkeys
lumpy with blood, their throat
that's me the way I feel

comical the wattles when they wobble
when I say something I guess

it flops there in red rags
love a thirst an embarrassment

rags on my face & neck a rage
at my age you can spot me

coming all day long the wind
chafes & swelters all day
long I pick & scratch
till my throat is raw as air
as welted

did I ever tell you how
every evening you pick

the scab on my heart
& the sky starts to bleed

&

inside yards they stand thin
-shinned beside bulky skeletons washed up
from mineral seas
bones to the wind

the backs of buildings
smash like loose shutters
shoulder blades torn off

when you step in side
whirrr whirr
pulleys turn on with a jerk
pigeons sudden with light

doors that once opened
light a hand waving
once brushed darkness from its face
remember when pullets would let the moon
down on small chains felt dawn tug &
pull the day up
yellow from their bodies

night and day the house talks to itself
listens to the brown light
thinks it hears dishes
the soft click when they touch
where the horse looked up eager ,
shuddered

sometimes it gestures
come back come back

what it is to be abandoned
sun in the eyes dust on the neck

house beside itself
filling up on grief

&

see you coming
a mile off for
miles & miles hollering
your head off inside
how dark & stiff it is
you look when you slide
down out of your distance
you are a purple bulb
a slow awkward descent
you are a blind pulled
down for the night

a boy scolded for sitting
legs swinging the table
sliding off, uncomfortable
& now you are going to
shoot frogs you have
your sling-shot with you

sulking

find me at the bottom of eternity
a dimple in the scheme of things
find me in the heat of my kitchen
time roaring in my head

flour milk yeast the sweet tacky
smell first powder then sticky
how sweet it is i say
boy oh boy are you silly
you think

this is the way
of all flesh
of all things
kindling /gone in a flash

so what's the story Paul

&
wondered whether if we were
given to words we would wear
so much ink on our skins
we would resemble sailors
and live forever
in the indies
in our undies
& out of
indices of wonder
among bright and clouded skies
we wore as silk
tie-died in an azure mediterranean

turning into sails and ropes
pilgrims on a grass sea
who tilt into a nutmeg breeze where it whiffs
every day a bottle on a table that shines

launch ourselves irretrievably onto the spice winds
full spray for the isles
they are as they should be & as you know emerald
watch out it's us & we are headed full sail
taboo or no taboo we know
what we have
to do
ta da ta da ta do ta do tado
the coral reefs the south seas cobalt skies
gulls screaming in our wake everywhere in the gulf
imagine we could step off the earth when it staggers
reach for a lemon sun

learn to tug at the pulleys down which night crashes
on which night lifts creakily into view

the moon blown into full sail into a shifty sky
daub of light on the rumdark curtains & flags
snapping in the night breezes

stars a powder we spatter with our bright breath

&

love that
the way their eyes are
their voices
low as evening
so black & liquid
slow when earth lets out

something it has been holding

soft swish
rain & hay together

dark :
except for the bushel of light
Joe Lawson has poured into a pail
& hung from the ceiling
the cows drink from

& now the veins on his arms
rise when he milks
the ping ping ping
then another
shush shush shush
& a deeper sound
the milk foams with

their breath their sweet
breath, the cows

so simple their giving this letting
& the sow her low voice puts up with the litter
fierce at her teats

Joe swats at the cows
languid as love he leaves

can see where they lose their large
heat he looses
into the night

the white quiet liquid he carries back
warm sweet smell
soft moon in his other hand

&

things happen fast
as luck would have it

a lock-washer sun fastens
the machinery of their days
so tight she thinks they will last forever

sits at tea thinks
they might meet at the sea by the wall
a lather of rose and lavender paper
stuck on their dreams
the lath-and-plaster surface of them
that would be nice
she would much rather find him there
he in a long woollen coat she and her leather gloves

clock says watch out
watch your step

the world is about
to tip and stop

watchout watchout watchout

flora daisy aster violet

yard a yawn of yellow
s/he thinks is yarn
a yearning for warmth

each dawn pills
a fizz of cotton
a blanket at the window hangs
every night pulls
upside down
inside out

&

this after he has followed his clinketyclinkety
stirrups across
the wood toward the hitching
where posts dowel the world together
their chink and rowel across the yard up the steps listened
for the requisite drawl of his approach
slow as syrup in february

& roots & con so
nants busy ants at a picnic
don't panic he says this is
no time to panic he is doing his bit
rounding up what little
bit is left
he said or i
myself that

me ,or we
tness the brands
i learn to bear
& flaunt sometimes when
they ask
do I play & I do
i do i do ido
id do oh in a minnit
oo do be dobe do
id do let go
let go on the piano
dopey as a cow in spring
thcrc in our little adobe all right
then think of me think of us
in our little hacienda and i
let go my heart hands my throat banging
an empty pan a tinny banjo
joy to the world all the boys & girls
i think some
times there must be towels hung
on the porch to dry
and no one could tell
them from lungs
pillow cases sun irons
all the creases from
day after day
the helter of grasshoppers
little lawnmowers yowling and clipping away

&

her upper lip   faint moisture
and on the step there is this
little laugh as if   there is not
enough
air in her & the

lungs   don't
know
their rhythm

a soft hair on her
face burned and   freckled hand
fickle air   in her throat

&

horses he was talking again
in his fly-swatterly way
about horses HORTATIVE he told me
mrs. b. **hors d'oeuvre** was
outside
work definitely & savoury that is
to be out of circulation with
drawn removed (from
the library)is hors de combat
how heartless i thot

circa

1933

didn't we know
didn't he tell us
till you feel like a fly squashed in the pages
wondering why
he can't keep a civil tongue in your mouth

horse feathers I wish I'd said
stop talking nonsense & read my lips
horse-and-buggy horse fly house

fly horse radish a little relish
garden radish horseless
carriage a run-away sleigh
bennett buggy horse-hair
sofa horseless marriage unbridled
ravishings horsing around horse
flesh a horse laugh hoarse throat
hors la loi
that's what
yr on the outside looking in

whores throat hort
i cult
ure hort
us con clus
is the shut guard

N the closed gate P

the last laugh

&

not that he's wrong
he's got a point
to tell the truth
i myself have been scheming
dream of never returning
from recess running out
way to heck and gone past the railway
junction recklesss as a runaway hen
headed straight for the river
smell of baloney & butter
on my hands skipping
my knees skinned &
dipping for snakes
skinny dipping with all
the young rakes

cock a doodle dandy
a dingle dangle handy
all the way to zanzibar all of the aches going
  and coming and
allen and andy and alex
                    i have laid
    eyes on them
and would it had been hands
they were such handsome fellows

but most of all
oh most of all
randy and he
me and randy
smooth as cornsilk
and who'd believe me he
slippery as houdini
up & asked me

wouldi wouldi wouldi wouldi wouldi wouldi wouldi wouldi wouldi

whispered in my ear all the way
to vernon train
jerking under us
past trees snow had
fallen into sweetness of
their breath past
the hard darkred cherries
hung in bunches by peaches
lanterns someone had hung in the branches
all along the hills
apricots with their soft fuzzy skin
all the way barebummed into kalamalka lake
in plain sight of the mackie place
goose-bumped with the water up to my nipples
hard in the air him too saying yes
yesyes yesyes yesyesyesyes yesyes oh
my god yesyes yesyes yesyes

&

small tremour in her
voice and her face
tumbles through like a horse
dreaming its skin and brain

prickle of work she's been weeding
picking thoughts from her fickle garden
would preserve them with the fidelity of a nun
/ pickles in no time

a jar hard on her
conscience as the hoe's abrasions
but she's bent
on putting them away
apt to do it
the rapture she feels
under that smell
sharp smell of weed blood

another you lean into
though you pretend not to
no no no this
cannot be

the sun the windows we are
reflected in
the tissue
our lives are so
tightly wrapt in

&

crow a perfect disgrace
        to his robes
dreams blue dreams
dreams he will shine
show off the sheen on his feathers
the way he will shout
it will be perfect
grind & bump his throaty song
his thirst for light for the way
it will fall on him suddenly
& he will rise out of darkness
birds will twitter across the floor
his mind has made in this music

crow a beautiful blue
in his mind a smooth floor
the whole world jives & jitters
crow the handsome devil
shouts his head off
crow lets all his pain into the riffs
croons where he leans
        over the wax
giddy with blues heart
full of ribbons the saxophones throw
over the room achingly
                quick on the skin
& the percussion ticks & ticks

crow cries when darkness comes
out at the windows crow
raw on love & smoke
leans over the floor
pecks their lovely hearts out
                                        one by one

&

and once
one day

going home
a new way
a fresh
blue
gingham

faint
whiff of

lotion

a little
extra
waver

in the
air

&

p pulls out
his timepiece pulls out

his hair watching over me
truant officer afraid

i will play true
and false with him
deeply suspects i will go

astray will miss a few days
spilled easily as an ashtray
has noticed i have grown
absent-minded & unpunctual
contumely he says contumaciously so

is that so
why not
ask me i say
i will find myself
in deep
in bad company
hooked up with back
seats and lip
stick come come
pleatly unhooked
shout my fool head off
i will honk like a goose in mating

you're right p.
im just asking for it
once they lay me
down to sleep
)if I should die)
im quite the lady

&

the parlour you swept
step now slip
pery floor giving
way be
neath the
steep

night a
sweet resin
the dark so appealing
against all reason
you rub your bones on
& your slip sticks
nonpareil you would say

all night long
under a pearl
moon you peal
off my blouse uncover
my pale breasts unbutton
bones in the dark
take off every bit
of my apparel
smear sweat
sweet as sin
across its silk peril

the barn dance
bone dance   you wish
you could do

every   where
where   ever

flesh jingles

the long bone
the five   fingers

play   from
play   on
every   night
touch all the   right stops

oh do   not   stop
& starts   easy as wind apparently
brief   as ecstasy

you think you haven't a prayer
here on the prairie you know
when you yell

it's a long long
way to tip
the prairie
it's a long long
way to go & man oh
man it is
such a nice feeling you
to the very tips
of my breasts

&

I know that Philip we all do
and it may be the thing that has
been is what will happen and what
ever is done is what always will be
again and again forever
& ever etc. without ever

it may be vanity Philip
but I want something
more I want something
new under the sun you want too

a little variety wouldn't hurt
as all along you would have known
had we but music enough and rhyme

though one generation dries up
and another burns up in green
reeds reels for a moment over
the ragged & thistled earth
turns to ragweed in fall
though it may last only a little while

i want rivers that flow
to the sea /to me
would swim near Vernon
where the sun drips into apricots
cools with the pull of gravity into pears
you surely must guess i would
live for waters that crash
past & through me
roaring
into & away
all the way to the Pacific

&

sd we have come the boy
sd sorry we are sorry sd
it is better the
boy sd sad this way it is
he doesnt the boy
we have belong this
doesnt the boy sd he
doesnt we belong sorry

the door sorry this
way for the boy sd he
are the boy come have
we sd he doesnt at
nothing this better way
stood sorry sorry
way it is help you sd you
cannot for the boy
sd at the door sorry
sorry we are sad
we sd you cannot help
the boy sd at the
door nothing nothing
stood not the boy this

&

dearly beloved   he says
    on sunday   the sun out
    in its sunday best
        dearly   beloved

sun on hot   so hot
it is a   grasshopper
the shrill when   its shell breaks

it is in the telephone
wires we are

the poles on the wires
strung tight as a fiddle
only we make one note
a thin dry note
& some one may be dancing

birdie fly out & crow fly in

the light falls down
the wires
we pass around
try to tune
ourselves
cut our wrists on

the whole sky should be an aviary
we should all be dancing
the whole sky moving

the sky is full
clogged with alkali the winds poisoned
the wells & we are scales
flaking off the sun a lemon
the drops fall on our skin
bitter & burning

dearly beloved he says
inside the white clapboard church
the hard benches the eyes dark from his words
dearly beloved
who could wish for more
would that we would
philip would that we could be
all our days
dearly loved
& loving

&

the stones where she dings them
rails ting and i think those tiny things
what chance have they
kids with dimes at the candy counter
church ladies ringed with spoons and
saucers
think: glass houses and I mustn't
throw them

well that's the way isn't it only smaller
that's why i wince when i think all those stones
hitting glass clack clack
the sickening sound

and i think grasshoppers and the telephone
lines shrill in summer
keeping time to the hurtin' songs
the air buzzing with heat & gossip
and gypsies for some reason gypsies

all the lines we pluck
a hot tension in them
something yearning as Nathan's fiddle
and the young people flushed
their faces hot and fast look
at each other and touch

if you were to phone
even once send a needle of sound
sew up the afternoon with a word
the day where it is loose & blowing
where it flaps loudly in the wind
release something so hot it zings
down this line i walk under
she and i talk under

she with her small white face
sends the stones
and her small breasts surprise
when the wind presses and her voice
for all her thinness strong
perhaps you might call me

your words might cling
stick to my hands in my arms
unkink my ear roll and clang
louder than a fire when they call
the men and the engines and their noise
and I know this makes no sense p.
but that is what it is
it is noisy and burning
and it bangs
alarm in morning

it is a fine line we observe
is it not my strange man
my man of the word

is it words when i feel
my skin stinging my eyes
burning with smoke

&

would be   touched,

like that

soft as

a horses muzzle

warm

, jittery

think of this

,you,

daily

touching &

being

touched

&

-

her dress a long silk
a martin i think
purple when she sits
papal also i think she could be
saying her matins but no this is
a person from a poem
we are people in a poem
the one in which i find myself
        so fine and so self
possessed is she who seems
to have shed the weight of summer

one who sits in small billows of shade
sheds the duress the shun sheds
is a violet in spring
the sepals clear with april
martini in hand
a peril of great price
this gummy day in summer

-

June 31 and I have been
        to the Queen
                city to see
    the doctor see her

pull off the yellow
peel the whiteness
finger by finger open

-

when she lays them in her lap
sunshine tumbles lazily through and onto
and sometimes it moves in freckles
    over her small breasts
catches an amethyst on the silver string

does she too know that inside the elms
a warm syrup slides
cure for the cold that has afflicted us
she must know her dog

is buckled to a long nerve
and that it trails from her arm
like a mohair scarf
sniffs snuffs snuffs at my dress
pushes a wet nuzzle under
smelly breath , hot body

-

senses my distress
her eyes with mine
blue for a moment
i think they might be glass
her thin face a
smile passes over
quick apology
her lips thin and she smiles slightly
the small pain in it

oh i am so sorry

is he bothering you
no no
no it's ok
really
come here gypsy
come here right now
more sniffing more noisy licking
come here boy

-

young man on the other bench
green i see the bench is dark green
sleeves rolled chin propped
just inside the light
his brown eyes

can feel him watching feel it
          leap from my face
the heat coming off headfirst

am a field on a hot day
the air blurry & shaking

feeling like a kid's transfer
about to be affixed
to another skin

sticking my beige
dress to the bench

-

the man in white
frayed at the cuffs the neck yellowing
said i am sorry mrs. bentley
smells of rubber and iodine
          you will be all right
    perhaps next time
says from the red kinky hair

-

i am sorry philip
so sorry i am
so sorry
                    i will say

-

is he bothering you she said

&

The flyer was a fast passenger train. Almost fast as the silk trains. They ran silk clean through to New York city, 60 miles an hour, non-stop. Blew through like a fart out of hell and the young guys they'd gather, sort of, to see 'er runnin' from somewhere to somewhere, wind and cinders.

But when they stopped, by the sweet dust of Carnduff, I tell you they were something to behold. Pull in, sweaty, stand there panting glistenin' with sweat

shuff, **shuff**

shuff shuff

[long silences]

Something special way they'd wait, eyes closed and breathe real slow, waiting, and there'd be the coal smoke and the hot smell of oil, the dark spots where it's stopped, steam.

shuff shuff.

One time she does stop, no zip-in zip-out between scenes, and out hops this slick-lookin' young fella, slick as a frog in spring, local boys 're impressed, that's why they snicker. Or try to, they're watchin' how he wears around him, real cool, clean past the water tower and the one-cylinder engine and its popping, steady and snuffled all night long, some way of walking. Cows gaping, who is this guy, small neat man past the water trough, right in front of the town gossip in duck-foot dismay, the pump in creaky disapproval, trying to clear its throat, right straight into the gleaming chair without so much as a jangle or rattle where old Burridge talked the mayor into a hot new electrical treatment for dandruff and his hair zapped straight up there was a tingling he said it was rather pleasant his hair lifted up to here when it zapped and sparked and set his boots on fire, flames this long coming out of his heels, day of the burning foot, traveller takes his coat off his way of walking hangs it on the hook before he climbs in before he says a word

&

this is in fall

flowers, their sore throats

paul so dusty
with talk
i should
rinse him out with tea

this is in fall
this is when grass
ripens to smoke

&

going to it is going to it is
    going to rain
        bad /really bad
there will be more
weather than in all of England
believe me it will be
a souser to end all sousers
a side-winder of a storm

a rain full of frogs and new dresses a real soaker saturated
with salmon and oranges and tea from winnipeg and
gingham from eatons and yellow curtains and a new
pointy brush for p it is

going to going to going to

it will let go one wild wash-out
the culverts full & overflowing
jammed with racks of dresses yellow ones with lace collars
and skyblue dresses with wooden buttons & ivory fasteners
and catalogues with red tractors driving out of them
and dreams of watching movies full of silver
it will be brimming with frogs that have grown
    confused there is so much
water in sloughs and ditches theyll lose direction
and muskrat surprised they can swim
and tadpoles that teem and squirt

one of these days one of those days
the clouds will scud like dust over
the floor of the sky
across the washboard curdle
awkward unadorned days wind
in endless cold and wet
a lumpy journey to rain
we the lumpen proletariats
lariats whirling around our ears
& hurling about our ankles

we at a calf-roping on our way
out and all the way back
one two three a larr-ee-oh
when them bump against the horizon
they rumble and shake
begin to hump up start to pump
their fists and grumble

night is a priest in woollen cassock
they make quite an array
priest and clouds
              when he talks
practically beats it out of them
              carpets on the line
clouds in little puffs of moisture

              says they have gone
in the wrong directions
wrung tears like a confession from them
and sometimes a confusion of wind and hail
in beautiful long scarves

it is going to it is going to it is
going to rain and everyone will be
standing around like awkward adolescents
              waiting for a kiss

&

dowdy did i say dowdy
                try dingy try abject
who could object
dutiful wife homely as a clay pot
just as dumpy & twice as porous
that's me, always some thing
in the way or unwanted

popped into Jacqueline's on the way home
some small thing for the wedding
Ned & Sarah such a handsome young couple
& I am to play, yes

some little thing a little colour then
& brace myself, their eyes

so knowing you know what
they are saying here's the preacher's wife
what can she want, fancy place like this

poor woman it's her lot
why does she do this to us

wanting all the same & determined
come on come on now
quick before i lose myself
swallow trapt in a barn

& the light i bump against can't see
so helpless it's a child
she's wakened at night & then the faces
& dresses coming quick as a stain
when there's coffee & you spill

& they move so confident they move
& the shock when there's the price
yes yes of course that will be fine thank you

                                        past those racks & eyes
& what can i buy for supper
what can i say to myself
what can i say

&

would lean over where it hangs
a hard light
swings at the end past the iron
rooms rumble by in rust
the dust from his elbows
building up in the caboose
he leans
at the end of the circus and blows
out the sun
where it hangs from his burning
hand rolling loosely out of him
blows the circuit

snuffs it like a candle
and there we would be
there would be
nothing but
darkness the colour of crocus through every thing
though the moon
would somehow keep on grinning

kathum kathumppp kathmmnp

a crate of citrus
it would ride by
cool and light
headed to somewhere
oblivious as a nun to cactus & cattle

the moon flakey from wind
the painted moon would continue
somehow inside its oyster shell
a toothy lop-sided face

and then
there would be

a waxy light
a darkness that was almost wet
a smoothness of claret
a clarinet that talked sweetly

washed over us
forty day and forty nights
we could get in on it
hey why not it's karaoke
and we ourselves would be

taking on water
taking in the whole noisy creation
we could float on darkness
listening to the croaks and peeps and bellowings
talking it up like crazy

over the cabinet in which you keep our fears
washing away the bitter light of our days

&

love that, you know, the way you wait
the way i slip past the last elevator
grim as eternity itself
as vigilant, and then
there /   in the blackest black you ever saw
there you are

a blood spot that goes
up
& then goes
down
& up   again
& already   i can hear you my god
your breath sucks
,night in

& in   ,
again

lie awake at nights thinking
red dot in your hands
the way it is
up & down when
you put it
to your mouth

can smell already
the wet spring the slough the nicotine
your hands smeared with the smell
the soap can feel the
chill on your skin
thin cotton of your shirt
the buttons

all I have to do is spot you
& it happens   all over again
night in
& night out
& sometimes   when i look
when i hover
on the edge
where town stops
I stop:

- fire
you cup fire in your hands

your hands
when i plunge
into wind & nightgrass

how sudden
it spreads   over me
grassfire racing my body
the hot contagion
till I am seared
with desire

&

HOWDY id say it's about time
you'd say fine swell dandy when do we
get started the camera
is already rolling what're we waitin' for
when do we get to dance huh
sweet sour feel of the sheets

[yr not singing
you'd like to
it's bin
perhaps
sing so long
gud to know yuh]

&

this time we are burying
a young man from over Alameda way
killed when his horse spooked

in this heat we rehearse our deaths
in horse & hearse & almost neat rituals

their ragged voices
trail through hymns
the voices catch & falter
fall away completely
break in thin pieces of cloth then
swell behind the line phyllis
leads them on

I will cling to the old rugged cross
Till my trophies at last I lay down
I will cling to the old rugged cross
And exchange it at last for a crown

how clumsy their singing
faith so simple so near
loyal as dogs, beaten

Bringing in the sheaves
Bringing in the sheaves
We will come rejoicing
Bringing in the sheaves

& the sudden catch
how moved you are
how they sing
with hurt & asking

you do not believe a word
    & yet
        you are shaken
     shaking
the simple power the way they cling
the frayed dignity
their worn shirts allow

real good sermon reverend
brought a little somethin for supper
what with the town gardens
      bein off this year

their own lives dried as the saskatoons
they preserve & parcel out
generous with garnets
careful with pearls

all their lives foreclosed
in dust & freight rates

the always strain in their faces
sun burns they carry
tight as harness on their necks

something in you too
surprised & not knowing
the naked leap of emotion
the simple yearning, choked with it
screen doors slam
when it hits

&

the back seat back yard ravine
wood shed hayloft ravine anywhere
touch me touch me
there
press me into me into
joy & fear our bodies
running hard
& soft together
wet horses in the night

the men at the barn waiting
rubbing the saddles
jingling the bridles
loose nerves in their hands

&

a certain muskiness a numbness
in us as we leave

the bare willows wreckage of reeds
a crow
his black robes the poplars
calls in disapproval

climb out of our love
something sluggish at the bottom
winter not yet toppled

everything we leave behind
the steep ravine the dark
water the stones
snow still on them

skirt wet & heavy with mud

&

darkgash in the land
wound dark thunder a dry
cry thunder the train bright
eye roaring sky cries under rain
calling trains falling dead
filling up with distance
circles into rain & calling grey
the mist we hear when the train
falls the rain cries into the train
rain fills up with the sky
us under the thunder falling
out of the train the eye calling
me falling into my head fails
the wheels going round & round
go round & round the eye the mist
my head filling up with thunder

&

a-men

aaa-men

aaa-aaa-aaa--men

ahh-hh-hnh-mmh

&

Philip at supper, you can see he is on edge of saying, tilts
his face toward the plate, his hands
stuck on the cup.
How are the Angers?
Hmm? Oh, all right.
The cup tightens.
Mrs. Anger?
She's ok.
Did you remember the pie?
Darned rhubarb is about all that will grow.
Mmm.
Mmm yes? or Mmm no?
Yes.
And?
Sends her thanks.

Philip wanting to say something, readies. Bolsters himself, jams a cross-pole into the corner. Looks solemn as a coroner at a drowning. He is a man trying to get a pry under a rock, wants to wedge himself out. And then he is. Out. On top, exposed.

And I wait.

It's the kids. Charles 's finally worked up his nerve to apply. They've been hit so bad they're living on potatoes, what potatoes they can get. Ate the seed grain from the government. Bank says they've got till harvest to catch up.

Don't and they're out.

Out?

Yes, out, that's it.

What are they going to do Philip?

Silence. Philip regathers himself.

I don't know. The kids are already out of shoes. Little fella's in these make-shift things his dad's made from old tires and binder twine. Maybe ok for summer, but come winter . . .

Oh Philip I am so sorry.

Philip, who says almost nothing. It comes out of him now, no stopping.

Charlie takes me out for a walk, maybe we were just walking, what else is there? We walk into the field, what is supposed to be wheat, and the dust rises like cement powder. Grasshoppers so thick we squash them under foot.

I am just listening now, he's inside, looking. Listening to something.

Charlie doesn't say a word, just bends over. Crop's yea high—no more than 10, 11 inches—plucks a few heads and rubs them.

Philip shows, with his hands.

Opens the hands—nothing. Not a speck of grain, the chaff blows away before you know it. Just like that it's gone.

What will they do Philip? What will happen to them?

Philip tells about Charles. Charles just stands there, huge hands, so strong he could lift the backend of a car, two people in it, not a word of a lie. His hands that can bend a tire iron are bewildered, they don't know where to go. He just stands there, doesn't say a thing, looks out, face so far and so empty you don't know what he sees.

Philip shakes his head and makes a choked sound, tongue off the roof of his mouth. He is looking somewhere I can't see.

Yes, it's bad all right. One farmer says the grasshoppers got

so bad on the Lang quarter they ate the harness off the
horses, cleaned it right off, nothing left but bits & buckles.
And then they have Philip for supper.

Squirrels, Katie says, lucky the boys got some squirrels. Got an eye those little beggars the way they can pick off those darn things, but she is sorry she shouldn't talk this way this is a mother's vanity.

The way they look at each other.

They are eating gophers. And Philip eats them too.

Shamed that he knows, that they know he knows.

Philip I say.

Philip.

&

desolate you said you would be
absolutely disconsolate if ever I was
gone you said my god you don't know the half of it
let me tell you you said i said it would be beyond

speaking a hole they could drive
four teams of horses through the moon
might well not arrive ever again
it could turn into a pot full of piss before
you'd get over said we could
wash away in the second deluge for all the good
it will & there you'd be high and dry

in your left-handed way that would be
the frosty friday the last grasshoppers
would hope they had hopped their last you said
inconsolable said désolée said absolutement
there could be no absolution for you

the first frog could swim forever & never reach shore
would forget land & get lost completely

it would be so long in water
its underwear would shrink to nothing
the birds that ran up and down the shore
sandpipers who studied the sand like snipers
could hold their breath till the world
up & crashed from silence as far as you were concerned
let the weeds tumble let the winds
breathe in & out empty bins inhale eternity
let the cattle being cattle have their day
being cattle in wind & sloughs
let the mosquitoes buzz our quarters
WWI fighter planes strafing our toes
so help me the hogs would croon your grief
if ever it should come to that

it is enough that the days pass like wheat
shuffling on sun and wind in their shoes

&

what about the part where he does not
withhold his heart from joy
for there is no joy in the grave
whither thou goest that one too
I guess you missed that part

oh give us this day
our daily bed

what about us
we may live in evil times
yet as the poet says
love will evolve
words bright nickels
flipped from his fingers
surely he said
assuredly it will
involve us if at all

all of us listened to a tall man
say amen says all men shall be

& though we are without
child and our bed is empty
our hearts abandoned as the red wagon
next door where it fills
with wind and neglect

though we do not
know how bones grow or shine
nor what happens in her who is with child
and though we do know
our bones will be ground
for someone's bread

do not chide us do not
say this Philip the dust seems
never to stop and there are
no fish we see so few birds

&

horses out there
grazing on darkness
night a pasture
they dream in, standing

& when they dream
do they dream of running
past the wind running
through an electric sun
night jingling from their halters

do they gauge
sugar in wind
gazing at the blue frogs
their dark eyes gouged out

El Greco lying still
& stiff as forever
strange grin on his face
ants cleaning his teeth for eternity

nights I lie naked
grass the sky full
eyes staring down
open as stars, as uncaring
the moon tied
shut with wet needles & thread

& days I fold
a sadness into
as i do your clothes
when I hold them

& the wire on the fence
sags from the weight of sun

&

dance night
the air rinsed
so it seems unrehearsed
& lean
bright intestine of music

moon a candy slips from your mouth
you feel the saxophone
clean as linseed & shining
take colour on the way out

hear it fall in yellow
puddles into blue

boxes step from the dark walks
want to close the lid behind
before you slip & fall

our feet fill
with music get wet
& then we remove them
walk into somewhere

you feel
between
your toes
you want
to remove
your clothes
peel off reticence
stand racing & naked as fire
lie down inside
feel your skin cool
& close
as forever

&

as indeed they do
the geese say

alas alas in thick-tongued voices
the geese lean toward the rain and
squeeze words from their cheeks

talk in the still night
the geese grieve the end

alas
alas
and again
alas

&

led my life month after month
yellow with dandelion
imperturbable as camomile entered
between cracks grew
legs so long and invisible
they might have been glass

you must have seen
: clump of grass   become a hat
the years had drawn
hair 12 feet long
in curls & locks
down the hydraulic of drought

: mouth a system of fluids
fueled on air
capillaries to breathing
blood to blood

something will surely sweep us
away I cry we will be one day one with the dust
any day now if you do not
jump up grinning windily & rhizomatous

the winds will come
& the winds will go
under an angry sun
the years will come &
blow us away

& you will weep over tea & say
no it's o.k. don't bother it's
only some thing
in your eye
really
it is
ok

&

except there wont be any
stepping
out no gal
livanting around no gal
of mine you can forget
that which Paul ever
gallant ever wanting says is
to go straight to
hell he's in
venting a broth
el a who re's house
get thee to
a whore's house
let there be no more
horsing around let us
rehearse our sins
no more a more eh

says he's seen
with his own eyes
how we get to
gether con
spire to brea the
how we two
gather to get
her the two of us
gathering
always gathering

oh no i say
i wouldn't
breathe
a word
believe

me don't blame me
you've got to get this straight
get this thru yr noggin
there will be no thuddings
no hearts slamming
against the night
against my door there
will be no she
-nanny guns
no nor no in
venting neit
her i venting

hyper venti
lating lately in
i cant help it in
haling my fears
i can't cat
chagain & again
such cha grin

youve got to wipe that grin
off of yr face you have got to get
this straight
got this straight
from the horse's
wear this breath now
big collar
round my reticence

&

this is my breath p.

broken

,for you

&

& now you have
followed your head
lights headlong head
strong through the setting
sun past the summer
fallow to your sweet
talkin boy oh boy cow
boy you have
gone & done it now you are gone
rolling your eyes like a heifer in heat
til you are almost sick with it
& no word of farewell not a word of a lie
that guy & his silktie buddies yodelling their heads off
sillier than budgies on sunflower seed

the furnace you have been
thrown into you move through
sky sprained open with sunlight
so intense you could sharpen
pencils knives scissors
the splinter you slipt into me
what have you
done you shouldn't sharpen
all the tongues in town
so sharp already you could cut yourself

imagine you a skittish horse
past the dugouts dead & cracked
the alkaline flats feet burning like Rachel in the bible
that's me you think goin' by goin' on down that's me
heading for new parts, parts unknown
you ride deeper & deeper into cowboy country
time spooling out in clouds of dust behind
hell bent for happiness drooling practically
past cockshutts banging away
clover farmers fondling dark-eyed beauties
lining up for him morning & night
their eyes liquid bodies arched
breath sweet as new-mown hay

imagine you barely notice my thoughts
in the corner of your eye bunching
at the fences on the way there
you think they're cows crowded up
like bewildered refugees like russian
thistles in sandstorm

&

& then lightheaded across alkali flats one whiff
& yr run mad, the sage, bawling, & you are there
waist deep in country
music you splash
all over your face laughing yr cow
boy boy oh boy
do you ever
wonder what you were
waiting for
your stage
coach entrance
the onus is on you
fog in your throat
wetting your lips
this will be a big
bonus the way you do
nothing but grin
nothin but
skin & bones

&

charter of four-legged thought
grasshopper rises in your mind

it is as they say for once
long thin pieces of sticks

the place that cranes leave
long legs sticking behind

they are dragging the day behind them
open or closed I don't know which

leave such an emptiness I know
rain could fall in

& i should be grateful
a wetness in a dry land
except no one
can tell
where it will stop
if ever

or when we will meet
hands apologetic, unsure,
how once they moved
not knowing
what to do ,begin,

trailed   swift bodies
naked as love once the wetness of snails

till the roads are running
with water
the ditches are thinking
/maybe this spring they will take in frogs
long-legged for summer
& mosquitoes too the big-eyed frogs can devour
their singing devoted as dusk to mosques

&

fast Vs & still longer

Ms he's learned

Ws make a quick

// flight

consonants in lines turn
back on themselves, that's birds
inconstant in life as death
vows though he is young it will ever be

a sky without vowels a sky
without rain Hebrew birds write
messages from god Steven
Catholic draws proudly
in an uneven wind, clouds scudding
constant in their probity
unhalting in rectitude

Philip somewhere between himself
Presbyterian & poet
beside himself
sounds his approval or is it hate hhunHHH
wet clicky sounds on his tongue
ttkkk ttkkk ***ttkkk ttkkk***
world's come completely unhaltered or so he now avows

wonder how he would draw
the sharp cries they make
the spaces between where they fly
unaltered unheard i imagine
the places they follow inside
consonants between life

they follow the men in hats
in the wheat what cries
the insects make

climbing up their throats
going down their long legs

&

face it :
you got to hand it
to me

i shld be demoralized
the garden so democratized
i listen all day to weeds
give solace to sow thistle
is that right i say talk
to ragweed friendly as flies

you can watch where i dig
& dig until at last i get
the dirt on you bury you
like a potato on the lone prayer E
the way you romance
darkness heave
caragana roots loose
unmoved by their clicks and cries

well all that, that's neither head nor tails

remember how my tongue stuck
my gramma's rain barrel
i leant into january
the round page of snow
laconic from
then on

in all this having
earned exemption i have
the stories i hold i told on my fingers
roll them over & over
the tips a magician
at the fair brightness
climbing up & down the backs of his fingers
the stories ive given you familiar as quarters, almost,
first one face, then the other,
wonderful as a two-headed worm

warm & bright as buttons on a blouse
  a pin in your palm for that matter
roll them up in bits & strings
            wanna drag

  there where the big dipper is full
              stars we could drink
rolling them, one-handed, over the prairies
chummy as they come

                    but dangerous
                    if you breathe
                              hard to shake
                hard to wipe off

&

in the basement potatoes
stare out of their eyes
fumble for something
they've lost some
where they're lost
the thick white meat
before supper i will lop off
their thin arms stick
knives into their faces
their heads lolling like hydrocephalics &

twist /one
by one

gouge out the pink eyes
squinty with waiting
hating their lepral passion
their being too much out of the sun

fill my pockets
with wind feel
through the unthinkable floor
its coolness
the spoor of potato bins

the preposterous white arms

logical as years
reach through
the hemp skirts
their drydirt smell

the yearning of basements
the country of my loves
a rough wandering of light
a fumbling to start again

&

a swollen head the dark squeezes
every night the sky shuts
us in the rooms we sleep in
& begins
it shunts on & on
without interruption

Boston it says Boston Blackie

tells us This Is WGN /In Chicago

The Shadow
it says ______________ titles ads shout programmes
& it says movies **The Green Hornet** news
brought to you by CKY

Dutch Cleanser
CKCK we lean to the pops and wheezings

hold them each of us one earphone apiece
knowing how the pair would hurt if you wore them
hear breathings from the sky that seem to come
from a deep well
they nose their way down the long antenna
till you think sometimes they must have asthma

it's not much as a listener believe me
& yet it sounds so close you could sometimes answer back
especially when i can feel the table
under my hands trembling

later at night it tells us **blah blah**
we tilt our faces in
put our ears to the smooth wooden head *BLAH*
it must get a headache all those voices blah BLAH

in the cathedral black sheep have you any?
you know this you can fill this in it's
up to you to do your part
till death doeth dear reader i'll show you
my best parts if you show me yrs

talking & talking inside
on the other side of cloth & lattice
what is this a confessional
& i think well why not he is a man of the cloth
so help me god doesn't he count
don't we get a discount or something
and it's a wonder it doesn't
go crazy & sometimes we talk
in smothered walnut voices

uh huh Philip says
when the brown head says
this should not happen
these are vices
this is not right
yuh we say that's right
we can do something
when it says
fat cats city mice bay street
says coupon clippers grain exchange
i say yes too
that's right that's about
CFQC in Saskatoon the size of it
but only in my mind
i don't really say anything

and later it hums
every evening the brown head behind the curtain muses
hums to itself solemn as a cello
wind stretches the whole wide world on KSL
/Salt Lake City
primes it with dust &
we find ourselves
stapled on tight as wire on a fence
sky flapping away in dust

& sometimes music
scoops out of it
in a blue & yellow night

&
says lets play
a little footsie
why don't we
lets see a little
lets have a little
looksee

i say no
no more
let's put an end to
false alarms all arms
out of place falsetto too
OO OOO OOOOO
ohhhhh
trains tattoo the night

give them a little
nudge & they telegram
home all the static
you ever wanted
always wanted

to star in apocalypse
but are you prepared
to read lips lapse into stutter
when my lips meet yours
sing a little acappella
live in the ellipses of music
unaccompanied as they say

&

don't be
so darn suspicious
the times they are propitious
hey we can do this
straight or surreptitious
any old way you like
any old time yr good & ready

could be & probably is
astir ajingle
the stars i mean this must be auspicious
when the moon rides in you hear
the sound of stirrups swinging
so it doesn't get caught in the stars
careful not to get tangled in my barb
wire hair snagged like burrs or birds

& then pretty
soon it 'd draw
closer the moon burly
in its big-toothed lopsided grin

hurry id say hurry up
your caution entirely specious
here id say here over here open yore eyes
'm here   next room what's keeping you

can't you see where i glisten
listen mister you could put
up your feet white & cold as parsnips go ahead & take a good
look a long swig my god set aside
your comicbook walk your buttermilk
gawk you've got
to start to talk sooner or later
about permission listen in on smalltalk about burning
think seriously about licence
poetic or otherwise

prepare my man for a grand larceny a holding up of hearts
if you play yur cards right you could
learn to become precarious in your season precocious in parts
yearn to be lenient with chickens ferocious
in dreams you should be
licentious in small things

above all you should think big
practice up to be a better person to be grand
arson of hearts
know in all things yours is a mission
your sins of emission

i know durn well if yuh put yrself to it
yuh cld pull it off

&

STOP back for!given come STOP
forgiven forgiven back
come come back give come
back come back come STOP
back ! come for back come
back come STOP back
forgiven come back come
back home give back come
is back come for back come
come back STOP STOP STOP
back STOP STOP STOP ! !
STOP home STOP STOP all is
! for give n for all is
forgiven all is forgiven
all is forgiven forgiven or
all is come all is all is

forgiven back all come !
ive given all is TO give
give home fORgiven STOP all
is forgIven all STOP is all
is forTOP given home all is
forgiven SP forgiven or f
org i ven for tops hoME
STOP is all POTS TO all
HOme stop all is you stupid
jerk

&

birds

migrating
brides of god someone must once have said
my greetings to you
the suns braid
the scatter of birds

dust whacked from a carpet
a drunk to the other side of the street
takes his gripes for a piss
fhfh

snot blows from his nostrils
rain & air earth turns its back on steps
round the sun its broken ribs

a rain storm
wobbly in the night pastures
deep with motion

\- ffh

&

birds shaken down the seasons stray
its shale face hard with waiting
a tray of wind
a path in cinders past the grating
man in a pub listens

sun a hot muscle
lets out a snort
lets out a sigh
& the stars ignite
the return of their breath

thumbs blood from our bodies
till the skin is loose
spider in the upper room
feigns disinterest we tremble
when she oils her shoes

shadows sit at the table
their long arms patient
a table far as we can see
moon its warm dough
its white stomach rising

cats form pools at my feet
2 feet under the boards my cold feet
white wind want
to blow into flesh

&

in the dream they laugh
& clap
drip into the dusk
memory tall as weeds

in the dream you have gone
          where men are ribs
and in picket fences wind hits
  they clack   & stutter
whirl overhead in mills
pulling something up your body

          all this win
diness my fears pass over
   brighter than dimes
whose saving you have dinned daily
hands chapped with silence
            nothing to touch

don't fence me in
gimme and lots of and
when I'm slee-ee-ping
you shld be we-ee-ping

lean men lean over their hands
seem to wheel water into the air
the dusk where it grows husky
      covers the faint
drizzle of children the low
raspberry of your voice

&

thoughts itch
twitch till they are
horses in mosquito season
grow smudged & choking
more reckless than a pig snuffing down flies

sometimes when I sit
                before myself
days thick as honey

can see myself feel my
self to the very tip
tight with expecting
I could
walk clean through
the clutter of flesh &
never return
never look back though
i could push my way through

suddenly shovey /showy with motion
ardour a door another door i open
& the piano is playing
in suspenders & cuffs

the clatter it makes closing
could be a hub cap
rolling away
my body i mean
hubba hubba someone might say some
young man in self adoration
darling he says
a daring thing he thinks
i think he thinks
i should simp & flutter
means to be endearing
though no one seems to notice
& who could endure
such fame anyway

I could)on a dare
& for two cents would
jump right out
leap from blue into blue
frame a camera going going
`clickety clickety`
lickety split
a windy mosquito shuddering
light splashing shut
behind &

& there I'd be
things beginning
to settle
all the lines thrown over
time ironing out the ripples

&

falls out of the dark
oops skooze me msrss benly

smell of it on him
night of stewed prunes

evn'nn he says & grins
embarrassed i think
thick with friendliness
lost his farm, poor man,
his wife too blown away with the dust
it's ok he'll snooze it off
the night that is

hello mr. aberman

& then the others, right behind
thrown up like rocks in spring
and I think most of
gulls, strewn on fields
smell of soil where it blossoms
stone faces floating
& they sing some song of the sea

they are pilgrims on the sea then
that or fishes
in the dark between the banks
where they swim against morning

its thin unbreathable aether
under a sheet of ice that is
almost unbreakable

their swallowed lives
boiling out of them

&

a crate of apples could i suppose
do it
create fall and before that spring
air of prairie in may
mayhem when red swallows
slip the sky knead it
into their houses
their thoughts of mud & straw & somewhere apples
white as snow already on the trees
dangle from their green syllabaries
chapters of worms & stars

what happens is
crow bars the way
crow spots a small crack in night
the lid dark and sealed with lacquer
pries his way in
beak & all
prayerful as his black robes allow
digs in &
heaves

breaks open the box light is nailed in

and it begins

a thin strip of veneer
on the horizon
by july it is burnt sugar

&
cool of it
a thick weight
big daub on my fingers

sees I look doubtful
here he says
try some
might solve your problem

RAWLEIGH'S
MEDICATED OINTMENT

for sunburn and
minor abrasions
~Soothing and Healing~

it says perfect
moon in your hand
blue & silver
you playing
doctor though you wince
moving toward smile
tall fluids strange bottles
we paint ourselves with
reflections of your care

if only it were
that easy
a can of salve, the cool inflection
you put on cows' teats when they're raw or cut
the petroleum softness of night
air so thick so sweet

craving a sickness i cannot solve
but know there is a small bone
lunate—small moon in my wrist
you can see the scars across
            a fear too i cannot lessen
more than anything I do not want to be alone

                    such care i think
                            & inward weep
                                     & later, alone
                    scared that i should be so
                        savage so intent

                                                         so close to cure
                                                         so help me
                                                         though you touch
                                                         I cannot take
               love's affliction
               an infection in me

&

listening to night sticky with sweat the brown head glows with what it has said and heard the air in which moths thud on screens light becomes yellow & hissy says uh huh talks talks through the fabric curtain it's hidden behind speaks in voices that sound certain listens in on flights of static all the pops and groans grow ecstatic and there are buzzes and rowlings and they make what you might call a terrible racket could be cats come from outer space the other side of the moon or birds they're that far off and all trying to speak at once so eager they talk over one another take over the room speckle it with their voices that spot by spot form a shell we talk inside a thin elastic the light in their voices warping

&

watching the Embury's
pull away tin can covered with mattresses
a future lashed to pots and pans
and dogs and kids coated with dreams
orchards tied on too with real creeks in them
and binder twine and chickens and letters
they will write back is it ok
to come home they will say
good bye their hands say & their mouths,
already softer

Eldon up in the driver's seat silly as a captain
coughing off to the mountains, over the mountains
a valley waits for them brimming with lakes and names
swan okanagan wood lake duck lake beaver
the wonderful names osoyoos vaseux okaha kalamalka

behind them the barn is falling to its knees
the bones in its back broken by heat & wind

they will walk in the sand
write their names
in the rivers the lakes the ocean

water so pure and so cold they say
you ache when it hits

house still talking
under its breath, bewildered
where have they gone why have they left
tables chairs beds all they gathered
their lives about
junkload of memories rattling
away to somewhere
good bye good bye god bless keep in touch

& then home
the slow wake they leave behind
not a life line in sight

the peaches already singing
the sweet pastel flesh
lent in the okanagan singing the blues
time is a spinning he sings time is spinning
and i am seized with sudden grief

and I feel as if I
am on an island
the last person left behind
and the only ship in the world
is pulling out sinking
out of my mind like a rock
know i will stand among
the high parched winds
all summer waving
dry weed in the garden
dish cloth around my mouth
daubs of vaseline in my nostrils
peering through darkness at noon

thinking how in this wild wild west I am a bank
robber I'd like to come alongside
sloshing a little

only I don't I have learned
I toe the line stand here where sun is
a blister
the bluster of dust a breath
-taking rose on the horizon
a pole they've taken the lines from
& i don't know where or why
day after day
saving my days up in balls of string

&

riding into sunset

you finally leaving

the engine

round your neck you

make tracks into the sunset

the setting sun

a rag soaked in gasoline /set on fire

telephone wires their hot intravenous music

the train follows its noise the nervous light

flaking onto night,

deep crimson of travelling

rooms, the stars stiff & staring

every evening when you speak

the world explodes

beautiful & burning

every night the suns wreckage

the edge of the world

blood runs down the worlds ruin

&

How warm it is. He takes it out of his pocket, inside his coat, pulls it out and says here, this is for you. What? I say. What is it? From Paul he says. I thought you'd like to see it. I flush, quick breeze, what does he suppose? Has he read it? The warm paper in my hand, folded twice, a nice firm feeling, nice in my hand. What can it be and why has he sent it? Mrs. Bentley he has said. Yes. I am Jimmy Ross. Hello. I have come from Paul. Oh I said. What is it? What has happened? I wanted to say. And then this fold of paper, not knowing what he knows, what Paul has said. Oh I say. Thankyou. His eyes a light brown, steady. What is behind what does he see through them I cannot see through though he sees me what does he know what does he think what will he say he said he thought I'd like to see this. Yes I have said. Of course, I say, of course.

&

denim & plaid denim & plaid denim & plaid

his horse under him jangled & squeaked
what if it did it did say yes
what if there is
a lot of pain that is
he's glad it is plain
to see the ditches will be
lined with black-eyed
susans in pleated splendour will plead
wide-eyed on tip
toes pretty
pleased to get a peek

inured to drought & talk
Paul crosses the injuries of time
rolling his lines with one hand in front of him
through sloughs through fences down ditches
he yearns round rock piles walks where the wind soughs
rides climbs in his studied way crawls scans stops
/looks /stoops to smell touch
contemplates more carefully than plato

a border embroidered with small flowers
in little rooms their parasols tuned
toward sun faces bright from smiling
warm and fragrant from turning
   their necks to day
they would die for one peek at him
all day their faint hum in sun
      small hymns of their praise

Paul knows he was sent for
knows he must watch
the Lady's Thumb the carmine ladies
are tough & thorny except
for the odd Saturday Night
they'll stand on the edge of the stars
along the paths flutter & blush they'll

laugh & wave & be gone
for another year swept
off carried away by men riding
in on the hot high winds
sunburn creaky & jingling their minds
their handsome way of riding
snow in their eyes a promise of cool linen
the edges of story where they come
completely undone filling up with ice

meanwhile back at the movies
the sweet things wink & jostle
want to get a glimpse, one look
from the handsome stranger
cactus & dust at their ankles

ha-ay watchet daisy

watchet yrself rosey this ain' no picnic

&

good riddance i think so long
but don't
let myself in the end *why is it so touch*
not really *& go with you*

riding the rods they say
& i think well yes
how I would like that too

a little scratchy breath
the short quick ache
stars fizzing overhead
& the moon its slow grin
all that unpastureized milk hanging in the pastures
under the milky way the bossies luminous-eyed
& unperturbed

lie awake all night long
thinking I am in
the night am riding
darkness to darkness
thump thump thump thump
the wild crazy want again
& then ka thump ka thump ka thumP

& then the long long wail
the cool & tarry tracks
lonely shacks that tarry
along the way blues
in the middle of the prairies
so piercing so beautiful
so utterly all alone

& then spasm

up & down
the backbone riding the rods
hard shudder somewhere
jerking to always coming
a stop

somewhere under the Saskatchewan night

&

should be
just once

three sheets to the breeze

but no not
in this wind this land

church sitting here
lone sail on the horizon
soiled from too much not travelling
stale smells from being closed
but who can blame it

too much wind
too much salt too
much day a dirty canvas
its eyes squeezed shut by day

its a sign i think

at night small lights looking onto
night rides its meagre faith
up & down the street
our ship rattly with rectitude
a wooden grasshopper in august

our voices on the verge
sing apocalypse sing against
their drowning
& still they're drawn, the people
worn and frayed faces
hymns like lanterns thrown overboard
a hoping to stave off the dust a few days more
ours is an anchorage painfully lit at night

it is not given us to ask relief
or expect
& yet   we lean into
Philip's words there in the stern
need deep as a well
we bend at, empty and singing

&

cowboy kirby stronger than the heat beating their faces a snare
drum heart laconic with love risen from winter
unstoppable as an artesian well
a desire for which there could be no cure or curbing
he macaronic you might say with verse

.o time to stop   no time to stop his horse says for him
it is quite an undertaking
& the flowers in their dimples sense something is up wave
fine silk hankies shimmy in their skimpy shifts & briefs
some appear shiny with summer others dusky in damask

faint with the smell of crinoline in sun
something moves in the skin that lines their throats
their ample and wimpled thoughts
line the street they do not know
he is an undercover agent plain & simple
can not imagine what dives he would take them to
what depths he would not stoop to
wince when he hits like a hailstorm

too rich for his blood though he knows
their routes has studied their roots
high-heeled kirby on the way to the Queen
City would like to reach
just ask us it's
Kirby the Cowboy is comin comin comin tuh town
headin in tuh foreign premises Regina where we could
regain something perhaps
see our dreams sitting
Mrs. B. a thin whistle feet up on park benches
at the other end, waiting bright as tinned peaches
a true thistle
perennial with hope just below the sun
wanting to be rose for a night just before my heart

&
moon her face when she steps
close to you close
to the windmills that turn the night
to the woolliness of light
the lamp lets out
bit by bit the globe
fills up with night

yellow as a harvest moon
the duskiness of her breathing
when she slips on
the words slips on the black
slip the one with sequins

this happens at night
it gets dark & so
slow and so smooth
it could be felt soaked in oil

when it turns up the yellow
the lung opens & fills

you can hear
when it is breathing

SS

SS

sss **SSssSS** SSS

is it warning or is it mocking
flame that licks inside the world's glass

the eye grows a little
brighter a little rounder i
sit inside listening

pss ppssppsp it says
wants to take you in
to its confidence hopes to confide

plenty of secrets to go around
ssh sshhshhs it says
talks brightly into the room

sometimes it comes and goes

thoughts the lamp gets wind of
and it talks brightly into the room
yes yes yesss it says

it has a wicked tongue
she thinks pleased with the thought
it could be distrust
a wonder it doesn't pass out from too much spite

from feeding with the grasshoppers on gossip
its round-eyed face in soft focus

&

yes yes his head nods
Philip listens intent as a cactus
the still wooden head
talks on & on

Philip bowed as never he is
in church believing the sounds
damn right he says

this head speaks to him
yes Philip says yes
oh *ab*-so-**LUTE**-ly
it could be a seance
this really matters

they get their heads together
the two of them, winds blowing past
Philip's small & black-haired
the other's large & bald
tanned to walnut from years of talking
goes on & on & Philip listens
like he's never listened
nods & makes sounds
the walnut head waves
its arms under the table
makes murmurs of commiseration

&

sucks on the pool of scandal
can't hold its tongue

perhaps wants trimming the way it grows
ragged and flares smokily
lines our glass throats
with soot we fill up as does the room

her face drifts warmly to her mouth
full and lovely on her face
makes a soft kissing sound
its hazy face says wish
hovers in a cloud of light
my doubts beginning
to dissolve like rust in solvent

i wish you would
you may wish you could
i wish you might

whisper up the chimney of night
lift the blankets that wetly smother
the flame i am
lying in

&

in the garden he calls

it figures wedge themselves white
as frozen angels blue as english
china they rub through grit all of them
lean into or away
you can't tell which

if you knew the four
winds blow either way they're waving
hi mom so long dad each of us
to & fro below or toward
the frame we are looking for

a way out a ledge to step
where we can flap like pigeons in wind

try to keep the door from blowing
away please philip we say please
don't you know it's us you can't
just brush us aside
you can't just up & ignore
our aches & pains are real
things have gone haywire
& here we are no thanks to you
stuck in ochre mired in umbre

now you've gone
& done it you've painted us in
to a corner &
what's the point
we're out of the picture
darn near

well what is he supposed to do
jude likes it she says it's good
he's sick & tired of us
who are we to talk
bitching & moaning he could take
umbrage at our age has it ever
dawned on us even once
he says with a sickly
grin i'm in this too he says stick
with him he's stuck with us
(i think he's stuck on Jude)
through thick & then this is difficult
why don't we just sit
still a moment why don't we talk
about ingratitude he can take us
places he can make us
famous make us known
for miles & miles around he reaches
out toward
the weedy horizon

but what would be the point
all of us here
huffy and indignant as stars in the last judgment

&

train drains the prairie
dries each town each day into a cracker barrel
wind a gray squirrel in the streets
track a spinal column
spavined over ties
work on the cpr & yr playing with fire
yr playing for keeps yr splaying for ties

spring where the sky is
sprained open pencil in hand
paul or the train writes
lassos in the air levitates words
lets say he is lash laroo & he stencils
little lariats of smoke & cloud
train tries so hard it pants & pulls
earnestly overhead
its huffy comic-book thots
till paul thinks he must be poet laureate

the world
tugs it toward the edge of

& every time the train
stops /
starts /
backs /
takes on / gives off
piss steaming at its feet
the cars pop
like carrots
for crying out loud

in the matted grass
the train passes flowers
burst into flame
trick it with their
short yellow farts

this being a western a real romance
Paul being commissar of comics said
& Philip commissioned to canvas
saw & with great pain painted
the entire & elusive cosmos from the first
convulsion, emulsion of mud in march
to the burnt-out ochre of days stored in August
till the last caboose busted loose in rods of sienna

the whole shootin' works
their thots burnt underfoot in grass
the purple cone flowers he'd read & left
their blood loud in the ditch
listened when it sprayed on the sky
dirty words that smelled to high heaven

&

you can see me now
horn-rim glasses chick-pea eyes
molting words as though writing were
a pillow-fight, the page a broken pillow

you can see
me at the table
march leans on
i must look a lot
like a plucked bird
dough white
flesh at the window
clear lens of its watching
me rising rising rising

sticky flesh the skin
turns to summer outside
when I pull it out
when i say
here p. have some
this is my flesh
burnt for you

such times do you see
under my hot feet the archipelago
the lava rock i walk on
my life turns molten & volcanic practically
i enter photographs of tropical fish & islands
blooming in the newspaper
i could have emphysema if i tried

imagine the table legs beginning to buckle
me scratching myself with the pen
the land already cracking
whose fault is this
everything beginning
to move
out to sea

you in the doorway
licking your lips
butter running from your mouth

&

sshh shh shh he says
don't fret
but i
can't
help it
so tall & thin
feel like a blue
heron a

going by on stilts
& the whole world
tilts
my feet scratch the dirt
when we meet behind the elevator
must think im searching
a pigeon among weeds looking for the seeds of life
my legs itchy where the skirt hems & haws
a few seeds i might find for him here
fine ill say help yourself elm i will say flax
wheat loving them in my mouth

& then when they are
they are symphonies of kisses
lopsided & wobbly   till there are
loopholes   loopings
i think oh boy i will
break
into music
unbearably quick, an oboe possibly
blue as a bone

all the right
stops
he touches
there & there   & there
he says   oh sweet jesus
the other words breathe
ing into
my ear yes
yes yes i say closing
my eyes a slip of the lips can
hardly
take a breath

&

need to take ourselves
talk ourselves off
the shelves like saskatoons we winter on
solve the huge pages that stretch to eternity
wagon trails patrol trails railways
grid roads telephone lines that twang
their western songs buffalo trails
huge animals rumbled over
their dust a sign once for 50 miles
left holes in the ground where boulders might have lain
each spring water marks just below the surface
& for 10000 years people would read them

you can see the bones & rocks where tipis stood
where they must have flapped in wind and in winter froze
was it cold as the glacial beds
we need to lie in and at home sometimes do

across the enormous parchment
we scribble shabby stores ram-shackle sheds
where they have drifted up on the shores of eternity
our scrawl over the prairie i think
is at times barely literate
a gouging of gerund
a debris of noun

the way we rub rub rub
breath over flesh under bone
press hot lead into the snow
furrows turning under bits & pieces of words
the skin of a place that will not cry out
seems never to ask or reply

send this send my
self my love
letters knowing you
will be watching
night over my face
curling up at the edges turning

black where you speak & touch
the sin in which we write
ourselves into talk
wetting our lips
our quiet talk
a low hot world
our bodies all over the sheet
lightning at night

&

a sea if turtles
all turn & go
one way back on each other's back
at night you have heard them
move in little bottles
creatures on a far green sea

the thickness they sleep inside
pulling pulling pulling
a theory of moon at their membranes
blood a memory in their soft hearts
slower than winter
horses in sloughs
up & down
the seasons shifting like salt

can't help thinking
the shut-in houses they wear
pots turned from clay
the terrible places
where their eyes stare
their heads the sea

screaming the sax
when the dance runs
over our wet faces
lightning, wet and warm

always at night
the same old wind
tearing the stars loose
the sound of it
green bottles
the wind blows
in to you

&

what do they say
what is there to say
in the sun in the dust
in the unsheltered grass
hoppers those little
helter skelter letters

in the shattered air
what alphabets do birds speak

the snow blows and winds fall
sudden as hail & the sudsy sky shortens
until we can see
shetlands trotting stiff-legged & cold
skitter over broken rock

what then do ducks say
do they still greet the wind with dusk
swimming up & down last year's weather
when they flap in wind like last night's laundry
when they cross the road
blasphemers who can't help shouting
are they wild

west characters writing themselves in
air & water & cotton
wood what could we say
when the old brown earth turns green again

&

night out there :
the plants fooling
no fooling around flagrant
chemicals of their mating
sharp odours they let
the night rain the earth turning
late moon on its lathe turns in
to a bowl full of light

crying across fields
calling out in ditches & ravines
me me me they shout or whisper
want the sudden hit
the horny bugs birds
giddy with light
carry their lethal love
letters back & forth

the seeds we carry away
eating & singing
eating patrick might say
& crying out

cracking one another
open in our teeth

&

why dont we we could just break away & run down the reckless night naked as wieners as feckless daylight clinking behind falling off in bright noisy claims why not its time for a change heres our chance day light under foot its links new quarters skins rattlers havent left yet I say let bygones be by in dust once bitten i say hey no biting the dust no biding for time you on your vigil yr vigilante face wont see us for rust baby we could make a run for it just for the fun of it my moneys on them two monkeyin around you can bet on that you cant beat that it's a long shot but what the hell

all the potato peelings I mean church bazaars all the aprons & ovens & drips from the roof the bizarre jars Mrs. H's eyes stuck on the window her tongue gray as cold porridge me stuck on you some may call it innocent some indecent me I call it running around that too hubba hubba bubble eyed to the glass all the stiffness in the parlour glued on windows you could curl your hair on the way she leers what she thinks she hears & still have stiff left over all the clunky shoes all the things you get used to the rectitude piled up in chunks only dont dont lets take them in tow we two tonight a stoneboat we drag behind you big lunk big hunk i say huh i say let them scowl we could be a scow practically trawling for pleasure plea sure we do that we're travelling for treasure the 42 tin cans trailing behind yakky & sparking so carried away we may as well be newly weds worlds so brand spanking new words so sparkling you think well they must be wed & wed say bye bye so long neighbours tata Mrs. K, with the bad itch the hanky she yanks out & talk talk talk the peacock fanny glittering with 100 eyes adios all you cellars full of eyes calling & taffeta who needs you you & yr soap-opera radios yr gummy face all you guys & yr gunny sack sadness be seein' ya so long suckers all you waggin' tongues pullin' the wagons into a circle were pullin' out fer places unknown hittin' thuh trail our parting words in squiffs of dust will be falling among the rattles and when we hit the big town we will be stars

spattering on the pavement just watch it eh let bygones be
we say our tails raised warningly becomingly behind

so long baby

sd mrs.
(May) B.

&

you would stand by the wire
a jingly banjo, sounding, sometimes a piano
in my mind a cello
thinking doors thinking gates
places moon has broken off & wind
fallen in pieces like cattle through half-melted skies
their way home dissolving in wet snow

fields slump with wind with emptiness
wait in postcards for someone

the small plums you pulled
out of your summery head
hard bruises hanging in them
ornaments on a Christmas tree
dry now as your hands when you picked or planted

real and far as the caragana
you water every night in your head
/ a picture you could stroll through
hand in hand through the yellow
and then the long thin pods,
their pale green fingers

brief moments of rain
in september even september
if it comes to that
your stubbly lines barely legible

there on the back of alkaline flats
skies strewn with sandhill cranes
the strange way they sing

reminding of
brief moments
gestures of spring
a swollen moon
you could if you dared
fold hopefully up
mail home thinking
of me

&

sounds of a chair
scraping the floor
on the other side
slow music a brown box
it has covered its face
against dust or recognition

hard to tell which but there are its eyes & mouth
there is the confidential way they fill with company
swell with complaint sometimes compliance
dishes clink & rattle the soft sound
soap makes when they move your arms
warm to their freckles
the fine hair on your neck

scrape scrape scrape `'mere pal`
smell of fried potatoes `'mon boy`
whh *whhw* whh
click click click his feet say

fly you brush brush brush from your face
bright glass light falls in, falls from
the way serum must look

man on the doorstep a large flat stone
round and pocked with holes, smooth brown skin
must have surprised someone in finding
shipwreck risen into someone's field

a not knowing blowing into my face
across the yard `awk awkk awwk`

`pock pock pock` mrs. paley's epochal leg
horns grazing on sun eyes harder than bullets
dream their stinking
feathers & dust rolls out
in millions of molecules
hold dominion in a way
on the way to a chique afternoon
with Mrs. Paley

my hands from water
small marks where you fell & scraped

swinging out i imagine
the squawk the door makes when it opens
a wooden hen when it
shuts with a slam

dangerous as the gates in a
movie & you sing along

[redacted]

[insert words here
dear reader: **fear not**
your favourite tune]

&

first turn in the year out she would go
white as a turnip from the cellar
a strange stirring under
& there he'd be guitar & all

slung like a garter from his bones
lent with this stupid grin all over his face
where you bin 's'bout time you showed up
one or the other of them would say

& when he'd sing those ballads the badgers would
climb up out of their cellars just to listen
                    and pretty soon
out would come the skunks sniffin' &
snuffin' & in no time everybody
would get in on the act, belatedly, seein'
          as the times they were achangin'

&

& now when he hauls out his guitar & hooks
his heel on the fence
everything holds still
there is the spicy smell
the spruce when they talk
wind dark in them & stiff
paul flips & flips the silk
the stagey way he shakes it out
red scarf he takes from his neck
grinning under his hat &

opens, eyes exorbitant watching
three crows fly out awking
wake the blue awning the sky has become

listen he says pleased when they answer
the jays braving it out pretend when they talk
they are glass flutes rusty gates opening or shutting
the gates of heaven water runs over, out of

& when as always she leaps
her feet race the red-faced sun
the gates flap noisily
open to a field of snow
philip there, other side, tows his hurt
like a broken balloon or perhaps if you prefer
a bennett buggy, the lizard prints it leaves
huge & heavy as eternity
what's the point
if he paints it he paints it /that's it

just this side of the grave
yard just before home the wall she will
enter a rubbery vein in the grass
a filament so cold it would open lesions

lethal as mercury
distant and cold as fermaldehyde

&

the rest of us in bright eyes
rummage among the garbage move
as if we were abandoned
machines at the edge of judgment
bones of dead animals washed ashore
haul out the last of our horse-hair feelings & heave
our tortoise hearts onto the sand

such a sinking feeling here
she's left me here this is
for you she said and put it
in my hands
could you please keep it

all their faces   under my arm now
inside a large shingle that's blown loose
sound torn from the roof of the world
the throat of a cornet

the house's eyes as we stand
like seagulls

already going
one by one by one
the spiders
have already begun their embroidery
have lain the first of their intricate gardens
plan to hatch them in the 8 empty corners of our hearts

&

so cold

in this white
i can see

& so could you

a dog in the shape of breath
the station the train shaking
30 below and hardly able
to breathe winter cracking

the panes open
with ice
sun in bright branches

have become a child's angel
spread on a page the moon presses
a face
up to the glass i move

my legs and arms
in and out all night long
)an angel's only child

& when i move
the snow under me
squeaks like springs

so cold i could
fall asleep
& sleep forever

on my back
all night long
i am swimming
on darkness

&

his land lady philip says
was all eyes all surmise all
he could handle she would

lurk in curtains eager
as a jilted fortune
-teller pleased to be ready in dust
decked out in must & reediness
never fail when
ever he returns
book under the arm
out she lunges
smelling of suspicion
book book book & she'd
fall on him /an angry angel he said
it's curtains for him, for sure
upset librarian and him with overdue books
and an inexplicable love of vowels
he's been keeping books & she wants
to know why
what's this he's reading now
and he calls himself a Christian

however careful he is
plain brown wrapper
the smallest shadow
when he crosses over

out she'd pop
brightly moulting
dress downed with dandruff

ravenous for smut is what the old bird
he says her eyes would be
crazed as a brood hen's

out she'd dangle on these skinny legs
scabby with rectitude & start in on him
hankies fluttering from wrists & neck

she'd made quick little runs he says
ever see a chicken when it's spotted a snake
that's her—straight for the kill

tut tut tut & you're a goner
honest to god & he squirms remembering
her shin-dig he calls it

what's this: little red hen eyeing
the package hopeful for nudes eager for
shapes that make
no sense her body runs ahead of her
legs hurrying to catch up
ttkk tkk tkk kk what's this then

yes he laughs & winces
there 's no eluding her
there she is hennaed head & all
she jerks this way & that
& there i am
scratches scratches she wants
to get the dirt on me she knows
something's bound to turn up & so
she pecks fervidly at any little bits
that fall her way

certain she's struck paydirt
when she spots the name
French of course first thing you know
there you are nowhere to go & dangling
from her snorts of satisfaction
sees my look says listen this is what really happened i
swear to god
she's breathless as a skunk a perforated lung
pink-eyed & hairy-chinned she takes you
down in satisfied clicks and gulps
I'm telling you
not i not i not i not i cried the little red hen

the mills of the gods nothing
she grinds you finely
exceedingly fine   in her crop

&

meanwhile on the posts crows squat
squawkey with rectitude
hard to tell which is greater
their indigence or their indignation

prairie poets P. says don't look at them
perform their squabble with the world
thin-shanked & priestly
wind deposits itself

the years whittle & paper their voices
sin piles up thicker than sand
up to their shins & ankles
until they are hardly able to hide
their bare-kneed rancour

they have charges to lay & they
bristle with suspicion grow
righteous with debate posit recrimination
negotiate rebates on desire

when the wind gets really pushy
they dig in like rocks
talk to one another
take it to one another
loud with incantation
so incensed they smell to high heaven
4 parts neglect 2 parts rectitude

winds have poisoned their wells
they say they will send themselves
postcards they scratch in long & plain
tive scrawls ive come to see
they screw down the air under their arms

&

&

& &

know in their hearts they are gods
they are black-winged angels who scroll
their sorry & sooty letters and the sky is
parchment from everlasting to everlasting

the worlds blown its chance
its not what it used to be
not by a long shot
they say posing in black robes
think they like it
taunt 's all
they have left

theyre no poseurs no way not them
its those eastern bastards
fat mallards

we could quote them on that

&

poem after poem

they fall like snow

fall down a blue hole

in his throat

&

s/he cannot understand
what on earth they are doing there
why this lingering this looking
so longingly s/he could be contemplating lingerie

take it off s/he says
take it all
take off s/he says this is off
as yr gonna git hey wait
a minnet s/he says this
here's a take-off
that's about the size of it
you don't have to take me
seriously do you
no need to

TAKE A CONNIPTION FIT
YOU SHOULD JUST TAKE OFF IS WHAT

and he says or she says
well yes s/he would
like to

\perhaps not
but it's there for the taking isn't it
you could tell herhis nose was
out of joint the cunning rascals

well there's no sense taking offence
though yr bones be rickety as march
and your nerves persnickety too dear reader
no use standin around in their birthday suits
chafin at the bit

dint think they'd ever let it go

good god those two
could talk

&

and then it is over the dance
grinds to a stop one of those
merry-go-rounds when it runs
out of music and you are gone
the circles break open
we spun like milk in

watch the attention you carry
with you present to others
as if it were all you held
and you give it to them, totally

the music still waltzes
through me the way your eyes
held the smell of us
I danced and touched
feel now where your hand was

and now these steps into new steps
who is this man who is this
woman who am I what I am
left on this side of dance
this side of indifference

oh pretty little red wing

& I feel something
stop
a carousel   the music
stall that funny
& sickening sound
when it grinds   to a halt
casual as sandwiches & coffee
people talking about the weather

&

he who'd kept the words
finicky as a spider
working on her lines
underlining everything she said or
thought hed kept his word

hoped they might keep them too
& so he plied her sup
plied them with poems
never lied to her not once
when he listened in on her dreams

copied them out by hand
steadfast as a logger
he was you might say
a persnickety book-keeper

kept & played
in the ledger his mind had become
the words to himself every night

when he was alone
stood a little less
thin & tall than an egret
edgy with regret

it was a hard thing to realize
a shame it had to be so
unfinished

to be fini shed
sure be sorry
she who could have been
fast was much too fast
idious far too melo
dious with melancholy
shed never be

lieve it or leave it
alone she said
fine fine that's just dandy

isn't it you about to call it
quits she wld string it
a long or him

& so she should
he would always
relive things could never

relieve the cold & heat
that she was he at
her all the time
in the theatre
of their lives
he could never

let go
when all was
said & done

never figure things out
in the end

&

this is the last straw
is the last straw this
the last straw this is
last straw this is the
straw this is the last
this straw is the last

this is the end
at last
at least
for the time being
it is
if it is the last thing i do
i say i do i do oh yes i do
the one that broke
snapt like an old shoe
lace a face shocked to hear
but don't worry
all is not lost
it won't

last
it never does
finally it will
lose its lust
re in the end

&

face it my friends
our days are leased
now & then released
we gloss them over
are you not pleased

as for myself i myself well
i guess you could say
I've done my best
no no there's no need for thanks

it is the least
i could do
it's not as if i thought
it was done
or anything
that there could be no more
not in the least

what can i say
that's the way things go
whether or not they are finished
way to go is what
you should say

&

something is bound to turn up

it always does

&

or so the story goes

The Kalamalka Press

The Kalamalka New Writers Society, a collective of eight Vernon and Kelowna writers, established the Kalamalka Press in 1987 in order to launch and run a bi-annual national competition for a first book of poetry. By using a panel of five national judges, all established writers and/or publishers, the Collective achieved success with manuscripts that were not only winners, but strong winners that have made a contribution to the Canadian national poetry scene, and have helped new voices to be introduced and become established. Kalamalka Press's winning books have been short-listed and nominated for numerous regional and national awards.

The book that launched the Kalamalka Press series in 1986 was: *The Possibilities of Chinese Trout* (0-9691047-4-X) by established poet Greg Simison, and published by Okanagan College Press. Christopher Wiseman, in *Canadian Literature*, called the volume "brilliant in its use of imagery, consistent in tone, cheerfully grotesque." Subsequently, winning manuscripts were published under the rubric of Kalamalka Press:

1988: *Valancy and the New World* (0-9693482-0-7) by Nancy Holmes. Don McKay praised the poems as "alive with their fierce hungers, hungers which often recollect and give tongue to the passions of earlier women, and arrive in etched unignorable images."

1990: *The Small Words in My Body* by Karen Connelly won the Pat Lowther Memorial Award in 1991. Leona Gom characterized the volume as filled with "extraordinary poems, never ceasing to dazzle and delight. They are poems about language, and the words are danced from the lips."

1992: *Worlda Mirth* (0-9693482-2-31) by Su Croll was short-listed for a Gerald Lampert Award. Kristjana Gunnars writes that "With a shiftiness unusual in poetic utterance, the poems appear to be faking themselves into a reality far more stark and terrible than we suspect. The rhetoric of the Carnival and the Freak Show is used to create a strange world we end up recognizing as our own. ..."

1995: *Solstice on the Anacortes Ferry* (0-9693482-4-X) by Sue Wheeler was short-listed for both the Pat Lowther Memorial and Gerald Lampert awards. Kristjana Gunnars called the book "an amazing journey around the physical as well as the emotional world."

1998: *You Mistook Heaven* (0-9693482-5-8) by Dona Sturmanis comprises poems that explore "the complexities of ancestry, relationships, contemporary life and ... place."

In addition to these winners, the Kalamalka New Writers Society published an anthology of the collective's poetry and prose: in 1991, *Fat Moon* (0-9693482-2-3). Saskatchewan's first Poet Laureate, Glen Sorestad, applauds the "Language surprises [that] abound in both highly personal lyric impulse and the sudden turn of a line or image. ..."

In 2000, the Kalamalka Institute for Working Writers was formed as a publishing, teaching, and research endeavour at the Kalamalka Campus of Okanagan University College. The KIWW's first publication was: in 2001: *The Kalamalka Chronicles*, an innovative, multi-authored community writing project, published serially in *The Sun Review* and subsequently as a chapbook by RSVP Press.

The Kalamalka Press became an imprint of the KIWW in late 2001. The Institute's first production was: in 2002: *'Who Lies Beautifully': The Kalamalka Anthology* (0-9693482-6-6). Tom Wayman encapsulates that volume's contribution when he writes: "The range and power of the contributions to this anthology are convincing evidence of the impressive quality of the writing program at Okanagan University College's Kalamalka Campus. In addition to these new authors' obvious artistic achievements, their record of publication speaks to their dedicated commitment as practising writers."

In 2003, the KIWW, in association with the Mackie Lake House Foundation, made available a writing residency. Dr. Ronald Ayling, Professor Emeritus, University of Alberta, was the first resident. 2004: *Sean O'Casey's Theatre of War* (0-9693482-7-4) is the product of that residency. It is also a new publishing project for the Kalamalka Press, the first volume in the Mackie Lecture and Reading Series. 2004: *Country Music: New Poems* (0-9693482-8-2) is the second volume in the Mackie Lecture and Reading Series.

Also in 2004, the Kalamalka Press published the *7th Annual Okanagan Short Fiction Winners*. Ed. Christine McPhee.

KIds WWwrite
(ISSN 1703-3020)

KIdsWWwrite (currently in its 35th issue) is a non-profit e-zine developed to publish young authors' work. Its aims are to:

1. Encourage children to read and write for enjoyment.

2. Enable children to share.

3. Celebrate children's writing.

A new issue is published during the first week of each month, with the exception of January and August. Over 900 poems and stories by children from 8 Canadian provinces, 31 U. S. states, and 9 other countries have appeared in *KIdsWWwrite.* Ross Tyner and Margriet Ruurs edit and manage *KIdsWWwrite.*

http://www.kalwriters.com/kidswwwrite

Digital Archive

The Kalamalka Institute for Working Writers is host to a Digital Archive that will provide accessible guides on writers, artists, musicians and other cultural workers.

Most 'guides' will initially be in the form of annotated bibliographies. Archive visitors will have access to a mapped terrain of the artist's career, production, and the community response to it.

The pedagogic function of the Archive is to enhance the Kalamalka Institute's mandate of quality writing across media.

http://www.kalwriters.com/Digital_Archive.html

Criticism on Cooley

"Dennis Cooley: A Checklist of his Writings", Compiled by Craig McLuckie & Ross Tyner, with additional annotations by Alexis Ratz
http://www.kalwriters.com/archive/cooley.html

McLuckie, Craig and Alexis Ratz. "Dennis Cooley Profile." *The Literary Encyclopedia and Literary Dictionary*. Ed. Robert Clark, Emory Elliott and Janet Todd. Norwich,: University of East Anglia.
http://www.litencyc.com/php/speople.php?rec=true&UID=5685

Lent, John and Alexis Ratz. "*Bloody Jack*." *The Literary Encyclopedia and Literary Dictionary*. Ed. Robert Clark, Emory Elliott and Janet Todd. Norwich,: University of East Anglia.
http://www.litencyc.com/php/sworks.php?rec=true&UID=15618